MASTERING

Competitive
Individual Events

First Edition

Reviewers
Lanny Naegelin
President, National Forensic League

Laura Schlobaum
Debate/Forensics Instructor
Osage City High School

Editing
Ann L. Nelson

Design
Todd R. Kinney

For rights to reprint copyrighted material, our warmest thanks to the authors listed in the speech, text, and photo credits at the end of this book which is a continuation of this copyright page.

Published by Clark Publishing, Inc.

Copyright © 1997, Wayne Avery and Linda Webb. All Rights Reserved. No part of this book may be reproduced, stored in a retrieval system, or transmitted in any form or by any means, electronic, mechanical, photocopying, recording, or otherwise without prior written permission from the copyright owner or the publisher. Proudly printed and bound in the United States of America.

First Printing, First Edition
ISBN 0-931054-48-6

ABOUT THE AUTHORS

Wayne Avery competed in debate and individual events at Wichita West High School and competed for Wichita State University, where he received a Bachelor of Arts degree and a Masters of Arts degree. He taught English composition for two years at Wichita State University after earning a graduate assistantship. He has coached high school debate and individual events for twenty three years; including years at Lindsborg, Argonia, and Wichita Southeast High School. Wayne, a triple diamond coach in the National Forensic League, has coached over thirty five students to nationals. He has qualified students to nationals in all NFL individual events. He has been the coach of the top debate speaker at nationals and two others that have won speaker awards; has had two debate teams finish in the top twelve at nationals, and one in the top fourteen; and has been the coach of three state debate championship teams. He resides in Wichita where he is in his nineteenth year of coaching individual events and debate at Southeast High School.

Linda Webb received her Bachelor of Arts degree from St. Mary of the Plains College and her Masters of Education degree from Wichita State University. She has taught high school students for twenty six years in Kansas including years in Jetmore, Salina, Goddard and Wichita. Her experience with individual events include small and large school forensics programs including league and National Forensic League programs. In NFL, she has coached fifteen students to national competition. These fifteen students represented all national individual categories. She has served as a clinician for dramatic and humorous interpretation and improvised duet acting. Linda has directed over one hundred plays representing high school, college and community theatre levels. Her awards and recognitions include: NFL Diamond Coach, Outstanding New Teacher, Employee Excellence Award, and Outstanding Kansas Theatre Teacher of the Year awarded by the Association of Kansas Theatre. Linda resides in Wichita where she teaches theatre at Southeast High School.

This book is dedicated to our spouses, Mike and Nancy. Our careers in forensics would have been short-lived without their love and support. And to our parents, Retired Major George W. and Eylene Avery; Glenn and Eleanor Bradford; and Maurice and Hattye Webb, for all the years of encouragement they have provided for our careers.

ACKNOWLEDGEMENTS

We would like to extend a word of thanks to many individuals for their contributions to our book. A special thanks to Laura Schlobahm and Lanny Naegelin for their critique and valuable suggestions for our text. A special thanks goes out to Mr. Brian White, coach at Buhler High School, Ks., for sharing his methods of preparing, organizing, and writing impromptu speeches for chapter five. Thanks also to Mr. Joseph Johnson, coach at Madison High School, TX, and the Madison Forensics Squad, for sharing their method of setting up an extemp file; and to Mr. Robert Carroll, coach at Merrillville High School, IN, for his willingness to share suggestions for answering extemp questions and developing impromptu topics. A special thanks goes out to Ken Enquist, Southeast High School, for his photographic work in the book. We would also like to thank Tony Figliola, Forensics Director, Holy Ghost Prep, PA, for his contributions in duo interpretation. Thanks also to Vic Sisk of the Kansas State High School Activities Association for giving us permission to reprint ballots. Thanks also to Mr. James Copeland, Executive Director of the National Forensic League, for granting us permission to transcribe speeches from NFL final rounds. A special thanks goes out to the students and coaches that gave us permission to print a copy of their speeches for the appendix: Doug Miller and his coach, Glenn Nelson of Concordia High School; Ben Lerner and his coach, Pam McComas of Topeka High School; Natalie Foster and her coach, Richard Young of Hutchinson High School; Miriam Nalumansi-Lubwama and her coach, Tommie Lindsay, of James Logan High School; Jennifer Liu and her coach, Gay Brasher, of Leland High School; and Sarah R. Bahr and her coach Kathy Falkenberry, of Caney Valley High School. Thanks also to former Southeast student, Avery Kadison, for his help in obtaining speeches from the state of California.

We would also like to thank our high school coaches Mr. Glen Blakemore and Elizabeth Ashlock for their encouragement to pursue forensic activities. Without their influence, our involvement with speech and drama activities would have been limited or non-existent. We are also grateful to be a part of the wonderful group of dedicated coaches who have been our friends and colleagues over the years. We have learned so much from you.

We are indebted most to the many students who have shared their lives with us in the pursuit of speech and drama activities. It will be the memories of your efforts and triumphs that we shall never forget. The wonderful trips to tournaments and the chance to observe your growth through high school and beyond will always be the most special part of our teaching careers.

Contents at a Glance

Contents

MASTERING

Competitive

Individual Events

CHAPTER 1

Introduction To Competitive Individual Events

• •

After completing this chapter you should be able to:

❏ Understand the nature of competitive individual events

❏ Identify and define the individual events

❏ Visualize what happens at tournaments

❏ Know who judges at tournaments

❏ Know the awards that can be won in individual events

❏ Understand and appreciate the benefits of competing at individual events tournaments

• •

New Terms To Learn In This Chapter

Individual Events	**Humorous Interpretation**
Forensics	**Poetry Interpretation**
Oratory	**Prose Interpretation**
Expository	**Duet Acting**
Extemporaneous Speaking	**Improvised Duet Acting**
Impromptu Speaking	**Duo Interpretation**
Dramatic Interpretation	

INTRODUCTION

Learning how to compete in individual speech and drama events requires two elements: a study of the events and practice performing the events. Without a knowledge of the events, you can not enter the competition with the proper foundation. In this text you will learn about many of the individual events offered and also receive instruction in the performance of the events. Be patient in learning about this exciting area of forensics competition.

WHAT ARE COMPETITIVE INDIVIDUAL EVENTS?

Competitive **individual events** are speaking contests where students from different schools are compared. It is a co-curricular or extracurricular activity in many secondary schools and universities. Students compete individually in speech and/or drama events. The variety of events allows for students with diverse interests to discover the events that are compatible with their interests and that they enjoy performing. Whether you prefer speaking or acting, you will find many possible events that captivate your interest. In some states individual events are known as **forensics**. The term "forensics" may also include debate.

WHAT ARE THE EVENTS?

ORIGINAL ORATORY – A memorized, persuasive speech composed by the student. Maximum length: 10 minutes.

EXTEMPORANEOUS SPEAKING – A spontaneous speech presented on a randomly drawn current event which the student has previously studied. Maximum length: 7 minutes.

EXPOSITORY – An original speech which provides instruction or information to the audience. Length: 5 to 7 minutes.

IMPROMPTU – A speech presented on a randomly drawn word or quotation with limited preparation. Length: 2-5 minutes to prepare, 5 minutes to speak.

DRAMATIC INTERPRETATION – A memorized performance of a cutting from a serious work of literature. Maximum length: 10 minutes.

HUMOROUS INTERPRETATION – A memorized performance of a cutting from a humorous work of literature. Maximum length: 10 minutes.

PROSE INTERPRETATION – An interpretative reading of either fiction (short stories or novels) or nonfiction (essays, journals, or biographies). Length: 5-7 minutes.

Poetry Interpretation – An interpretative reading of a poem or a collection of poems unified by theme. Length: 5-7 minutes.

DUET ACTING – A memorized acting exercise presented by two students from a work of literature. Maximum length: 10 minutes.

IMPROVISED DUET ACTING – An improvisational acting exercise by two students who create a scene after drawing a topic. Maximum length: 7 minutes.

DUO INTERPRETATION – A memorized acting exercise performed by two students from a work of literature. Maximum length: 10 minutes.

The preceding events are explained in each chapter of this text. You should understand that there are other events that may be offered in your state. An exciting aspect of individual events competition is the variety of original events throughout the nation. However, there are similarities in technique that are used in the performance of most individual events.

WHAT HAPPENS AT TOURNAMENTS?

Inter-school competitive individual events are held at individual events tournaments. There can be from 8 to 30 schools competing, depending on the number of schools competing in your state. There may be 150 to 400 total entries in all of the categories of competition. The host school determines the number of schools and the number of entries that will be allowed for competition.

Students normally compete in one or more events, depending on state and tournament rules. You will present each event in each of the preliminary rounds. There may be two or more preliminary rounds. You will be ranked by the judge or judges from 1 to 6, depending on the number of contestants. The best rank is a "1" followed by the two, three, four, five, and six. The judge may also evaluate the quality of your performance through quality points; with higher quality points indicating the strongest performance. The rank clarifies who is best in the round, while the quality points indicate the quality of performance in the round. Judges will also write comments, pointing out the best aspects of your performance and making suggestions for improvement.

At the end of the preliminary rounds, the ranks are added. The six students in each event who have the lowest total ranks will compete in the final round to determine first through sixth place. At larger tournaments the top twelve will advance into semifinals. The top six semifinalists will then advance to the finals. The final placing is either determined by the ranks of the judges in the final round exclusively or through the adding of cumulative scores from the preliminary rounds and final rounds.

After the finals an awards assembly is presented showcasing the finalists in each event. The tournament director calls all finalists to the stage and announces sixth through first place. Medals are presented to all finalists. Sweepstakes trophies are presented to the schools with the highest team performance. Each student earns sweepstakes points for the school through the ranking system. The higher your ranks, the more sweepstakes points you earn for the school. The awards assembly for individual events tournament provides a fitting conclusion to the weekend's forensics activities. Whether you are a medalist or not, remember that the main reason for participating in individual events competition is to learn. The skills you will gain will last a lifetime. There are no losers in individual events competi-

tion. By paying close attention to the event expectations explained in this text, you will have a worthwhile experience in individual events competition.

WHO JUDGES AT TOURNAMENTS?

Individual events competitors are judged by forensics coaches, members of the community, college students, and former individual events competitors from the area. At larger tournaments there may be many inexperienced judges recruited from the community. These are referred to as "lay" judges. Some tournaments pay judges and can be more selective. Experienced or not, judges enable the competition to take place. Students should have and show respect for all judges. After all, a judge is offering his or her free time to provide feedback to individual events competitors. Through comments provided by judges, you can hone your skills as a speaker or actor.

WHAT WILL BE THE CRITERIA FOR JUDGING?

There are many areas of consideration when it comes to judging. Students are judged primarily on what they say and how they say it, or content and delivery. In speech events, judges evaluate content in terms of originality, organization, quality of research, and use of language. The delivery is evaluated in terms of voice and diction, physical expression such as eye contact and gestures, and enthusiasm.

In the dramatic events, students are judged on the choice and interpretation of the literature. Is the selection challenging? Does it have literary merit? Judges also evaluate the performance. Does the student comprehend the selection? Is the performer's voice and diction acceptable? Is the performer poised and confident?

Each event will have unique expectations. Study the chapters pertaining to your main events. Refer also to Appendix H of this book for sample ballots. An examination of ballots will give you an idea of what judges will consider in evaluating your presentation of individual events.

WHO IS IN THE AUDIENCE?

Competitors in individual events do not generally perform in front of large audiences. At most tournaments you will have from one to three judges and some of the other contestants in your round. Therefore, the audience is much smaller than you would encounter in a speech or English class presentation. The judges and fellow performers will be supportive of your presentation. Judges realize that individual events competitions are learning experiences for students. You will improve after each tournament. Participation in individual events competition should be viewed as an intellectual challenge for speakers and as a dramatic exercise for actors and actresses.

If you make the finals in an event, there will be a larger audience. Students often watch the finalists to get ideas for improvement. After some experience in final rounds, you will learn to focus on your performance and should not experience anxiety about an audience. Within time you will feel proud to be a participant in the final round. Confidence will be gained through the experience of preliminary and final round performances.

WHAT IS THE ATMOSPHERE LIKE AT INDIVIDUAL EVENTS TOURNAMENTS?

When you attend your first tournament, you will be in awe of the world of forensics. In the halls you will observe students talking to lockers or walls. You will see actors performing for imaginary audiences in stair wells or other private places. You will sense that your fellow competitors are serious about the competition.

Unlike debate tournaments students can sometimes watch fellow squad members perform. This enhances squad unity and builds strong friendships. There is often time between rounds and at lunch to socialize with members of other squads. You will enjoy knowing students from other schools. It is a fringe benefit of individual events competition.

By the end of your first tournament, you will have learned much about yourself and the world around you. Like past participants in forensics, you will go home knowing that you spent your time wisely, cultivating skills that will last a lifetime.

WHY INDIVIDUAL EVENTS?

Participation in individual events competition will be beneficial for you. For speech participants you will learn about the world around you. Orators will identify problems and solutions for our most pressing problems. Extemporaneous speakers will learn to analyze the political and social concerns of the United States and other countries. Expository speakers will become enlightened on the many aspects of contemporary life.

For students of theater, you will gain much though competitive drama events. Learning to present a believable scene without the aid of stage props, lighting, costume, and makeup, will be invaluable. Many auditions for community theater and college productions are held on empty stages. Your acting ability must be noticeable by the casting director, without enhancements. You will also develop a body of material through participation in dramatic and humorous interpretation that can be performed for college scholarships. You will stand out over fellow thespians who have only acted on stage. Readers of poetry and prose will develop skills in understanding and communicating literature that few will have in college literature classes.

From your involvement with forensics activities, you will develop poise, confidence, and effective oral communication skills. You will also possess a heightened awareness of current events, an appreciation for good literature, and a belief that problems must be discussed and subsequently solved. You will truly be an informed citizen, making intelligent decisions about your career, family, and the world around you.

A FINAL WORD OF WISDOM

Be patient as you study and perfect competitive individual events. You will not learn the theory nor develop the performance skills overnight. Like all new activities, it will take time. Place your emphasis on getting involved. You will learn much from participating in tournaments. Do not get upset if your scores are not competitive, especially during the first year. Through perseverance, they will improve. Success can be achieved by studying the text, listening to advice from your coach, and hard work and determination. Strive to win, but never forget the primary reason for competing in individual events is to learn.

PART ONE

Original Oratory
Extemporaneous Speaking
Expository
Impromptu Speaking

SPEECH EVENTS

CHAPTER 2

Original Oratory

· ·

After completing this chapter you should be able to:

❏ Realize the advantages of competing in oratory

❏ Define original oratory and understand the goals of oratory

❏ Know guidelines for selecting a topic

❏ Understand how people are persuaded

❏ Utilize methods of organization

❏ Know and use effective techniques of oratorical delivery

New Terms To Learn In This Chapter

Ethos

Problem—Solution

Pathos

Logos

Motivated Sequence

AN INTRODUCTION TO
THE WORLD OF PERSUASION

In a world of controversy, you are constantly bombarded with persuasive messages. You rise in the morning to be greeted by TV news commentators and newspaper journalists giving their perspectives on today's news. You go to school and hear messages about the importance of education for a successful life. Your peers tell you about the advantages of a new car or how John is not really a true friend. You watch television at home and hear mixed messages about our society. A political commentator tells you how bad the President is for the country while the President's press secretary tells you why the commentator is wrong. A report on the six o'clock news reveals the growing increase in juvenile crime while the nine o'clock news special explains how young criminals are unfairly taken advantage of by the juvenile justice system. You conclude the day by watching Ted Koppel analyze yet another problem facing our complex society. You go to bed in a state of utter confusion, either feeling helpless about societal problems, or becoming apathetic, never knowing what can or should be done about this troubled world.

While this paints a negative picture, a bright spot becomes readily apparent. In a democratic society we are entitled to freedom of speech. And the best way to vent our frustration with this world is to give a speech about it. Many of us felt a sense of exhilaration when giving our first persuasive speech in high school. After all, we had spent our entire lives listening to parents and teachers present their views of the world, and now we finally had a chance to share ours. No one would argue back, not our friends nor our teacher. This was a chance to tell the world what we thought. And whether anyone thought we were right or wrong, it didn't make a bit of difference. And it was this feeling that propelled us into speech activities, especially oratory. In oratory, you can present your own original thoughts and share the values that you hold dearly in your mind and heart. Wow, what a chance to exercise your freedom as an American and what a chance to make a difference in this world!

WHY ORATORY?

Are there valid reasons to compete in oratory?

Perhaps the most difficult and one of the most common situations for public speaking revolves around the art of persuasion. In our personal lives we experience situations that demand persuasive skills. In high school you have to persuade dad not to ground you for breaking curfew or getting a low grade in chemistry. Suppose you have decided to break up with your girl or boy friend, what will you say? If you have a job, you might have to persuade fellow workers to resolve an issue at work your way. Life is simply full of situations that demand persuasive skills.

In college or in the work place, the ability to articulate and persuade is critical. Without it, you can be manipulated by others' views and hold your real opinions inside. Doctors contend that keeping feelings and ideas inside is unhealthy. And if you have higher aspirations involving any kind of leadership, the art of persuasion separates the highly successful leaders from the rest of the field. Let's face it. Those who can articulate their thoughts persuasively can change the world. They are the ones who can have real impact upon people and ultimately society. Therefore, your participation in oratory can have a lasting impact on your life and the world in which you live. So decide! Do you want to be a leader or a follower? We hope you said a leader, because the world is in dire need of inspiring leaders to shape the future.

As a competitor in oratory, you will learn how to persuade. By writing a speech that your audience appreciates and prefers, you will accomplish that goal. On the ballot your judges will comment on the content of the speech and the presentation of the speech. If they give you a good rank, you will know that your speech topic and presentation were accepted by the audience. The fact that your score was higher than five other orators, may document your skill in this event. However, your purpose is not just to get a good rank. Few speakers receive consistently high scores. Comments are a better reflection of your success. Audiences often admire a speaker even though they may not give him or her the highest rank. Through your participation in oratory, your skills will improve even if you do not win medals or trophies. By studying this event carefully before participating, you can learn to reach your audience in a positive manner and experience much success as an orator.

WHAT IS ORIGINAL ORATORY?

There are many definitions of this event. In the simplest of terms, an oration is defined as a speech through which a speaker attempts to persuade the audience to his or her viewpoint on an issue. Historically, speakers have picked controversial issues and have taken a stand on one side or the other. However, this approach has risks unless it is handled carefully. A good speaker with a good speech can overcome an opposing reaction from a member of the audience. Essentially all persuasive speeches must be handled in a delicate and strategic manner. Suppose you are writing about the dangers of smoking cigarettes and how a smoker's rights should be curtailed. If your judge is an ardent smoker, the challenge of the persuasive task is heightened. This judge may even want you to hurry up and give the speech so he or she can go out for a smoke break. We often enter oratory wanting to believe that others see the world as we do. But we learn that there are many perspectives on issues. The successful orator writes the speech realizing the diversity of thought that exists in humankind.

Many experts believe that a good oration has **universal appeal**. That is to say, each of us is impacted by the subject. The speaker must articulate solutions that we can enact to alleviate the problem. Also, a simple topic such as patriotism tries to heighten our feelings and thoughts on the necessity of patriotism. This topic could apply to Americans, as well as citizens of other countries. In other words, the topic has a universal application to all potential audience members.

Another brand of oratory involves selecting an **abstract topic** such as hope, honesty, or fear. In such speeches the speaker selects examples from his or her personal life, as well as national or international incidents, to bring the abstract concept into concrete terms for anyone to understand. Again, the universality aspect applies to this type of speech.

Other speeches set out to develop a problem and offer concrete solutions to the problem. These speeches often depict a societal problem such as discrimination. They are excellent forms of oratory for beginning speakers because the focus is narrow. This type of speech allows the beginning speaker to cultivate skills in persuasion with a topic that he or she understands both emotionally and intellectually.

Many students choose orations that are based on **personal experiences**. In other words, their own experiences prompt the writing of the speech.

Because of self-interests and personal experiences, these orations can have a powerful effect on an audience.

Ultimately, oratory is very open ended. The fact that oratory is known as original oratory implies the necessity of originality. Although there are expectations, there is much room for one's own approach. This is what makes original oratory one of the most personal events in competitive speech. You will find this event very rewarding because audiences are waiting for the originality that you possess.

GOALS OF ORATORY

Orators try to communicate a **specific problem** to the audience. It may be a lack of morality or the need for more equitable laws for citizens. Orators also try to either create an emotional and intellectual response in their audience or simply to deepen an existing feeling or thought on the topic. The latter is more difficult, but both objectives are acceptable. Orators often try to motivate audiences to act upon a problem. Not only should the audience agree with the speaker, but they should leave with a desire and the knowledge to facilitate the action needed to solve a societal problem. Actuating the audience is the most difficult goal of oration, but is very common in real world speeches such as fund raising for needy children. Ultimately, the orator combines pertinent research, emotional appeals, and an appeal for action in achieving the goals of original oratory.

The speech should be written using carefully chosen words and phrases. The language should be crafted to appeal to listeners in both every day language and figurative language. Oratory should be presented with a sincere and passionate delivery. An orator should be speaking on a topic that comes from the heart and mind. If the speaker believes in the content, then it is easier to develop the oratorical skill required to make the presentation meaningful and realistic to the audience.

The objectives of oratory are not achieved by accident. The goals are met through careful planning of one's speech and a fundamental understanding of the nature of persuasion.

GUIDELINES FOR ORIGINAL ORATORY

Rules governing oratory may differ somewhat from state to state. Check with your coach before writing your rough draft. It could save you a great deal of time and energy. A careful examination of your state guidelines is necessary. After all, meeting specific rules is very important in any type of competitive endeavor.

Oratory is an original speech that typically falls within a ten-minute time limit. If your state does not have a minimum time limit, eight minutes is the accepted norm for minimum time. Many experts agree that a speaker should deliver the speech at about 115-135 words per minute. If you are a debater, you will discover that the rate of speech is much, much slower than a debate speech. Most extempers also speak too rapidly when first attempting oratory. The delivery of the oration should parallel the content of the speech. Sincerity can seldom be demonstrated by rushing through the presentation. You must deliver an oration with conviction, a sense of dramatic timing, and appropriate emphasis of key words and phrases.

The National Forensic League, a national organization created for the support and development of debate and speech activities, sets a guideline of quoted material at 150 words in the speech. This refers to specific quotations, poems, or anything else that is quoted directly. Even if your school is not affiliated with NFL, this guideline is a good rule to follow. Otherwise, original oratory becomes a term paper read aloud. Without limits on quoted material, the likelihood of plagiarism is increased. If one takes much of the speech from other sources, it is no longer original. The best oration comes from one's mind and heart. Winning orators are very original. It is difficult to present another's ideas with passion and conviction.

Finally, read a sample ballot from your state. Many ballots highlight important areas that judges will use to evaluate your speech and presentation. If your coach does not have copies, contact your state activities or speech association for sample ballots. Other directors of forensics in the area can also be helpful in sharing representative ballots of original oratory. See Appendix H for sample ballots.

The most critical decision you will have to make is the selection of the topic. A good speaker with a weak topic will not win in oratory. Therefore, it is important to give careful consideration to topic selection. Do not panic! Through the understanding of some simple guidelines, you can make an educated decision on your oratory topic. Try to meet a deadline for the topic selection with the approval of your instructor. Indecisiveness has caused many students to fail to get adequately prepared for the early tournaments. So begin right away!

WHAT TYPES OF TOPICS ARE LEGITIMATE?

Orations may be centered on problems; they may offer solutions to such problems; or they may be inspirational. There are many ways one can go in topic selection. Follow the advice of your coach before choosing a topic. What works in the final round of NFL nationals or the state finals, may not work for you. Students often attempt to mimic what was done at a previous national tournament either in the topics they choose or the way they deliver the speech. As coaches, we have found it apparent that students using this method were not writing from their heart and soul. Writing the oratory was simply an intellectual exercise. The result: many of them were unsuccessful at invitational tournaments. We soon learned that students should follow their own interests in picking topics, especially novice speakers. When students follow their own interests, they experience more success and feel better about their participation in oratory. Remember, national champions seldom begin oratory by writing a championship speech. They learn how to appeal to their audience through competition. On the following page are some general guidelines to consider in selecting a topic.

GENERAL GUIDELINES FOR ORATORY TOPIC SELECTION

1. **Choose a topic that is meaningful to you.** That is, a topic that you like. Perhaps you have experienced this topic in your life or know people who have faced it. Students and coaches who worry solely about what judges will buy may miss topics that are inherently apparent in the mind and heart of the student. The obvious topic may be the best. The topic that truly interests you will be one in which you can best convey its importance to the judge.

2. **Select topics that do not alienate your judges.** For example, if you favor lowering the drinking age to 18, you may not get widespread support from those over 21 who are judging. In other words, you are making your task more difficult. Try to avoid issues on which people are sharply divided. Issues such as abortion and capital punishment are examples. Either way you go, you will have judges who are philosophically opposed to your stance. There are such topics that do not ask an audience to change their viewpoints, but to see the other side. If you approach them in that manner, then you reduce the risk of automatically turning off a judge. Hopefully, they will not let personal opinions affect their evaluation of the round. Realize, though, if you don't convince them of your perspective, your effectiveness as an orator is limited.

3. **Select topics that have importance and definite ramifications on our society and the world.** Although you should be careful not to alienate your judge, you should not be afraid of tackling controversial issues. Many issues need fresh perspectives. Some problems may be so new that judges will not know much about them. Therefore, oratory succeeds by creating awareness in the audience. Although some topics invite debate from the judges, topics handled with originality and freshness are respected by judges. Do not feel you have to run from controversy. By writing an expository speech with a slight message, you may miss the purpose of original oratory altogether. Such a speech may come across as a cop out or a failure to tackle a substantial problem.

4. **Begin by brainstorming.** Make a list of topics. Divide them into categories. What problems concern you the most? What qualities bother you about individuals within our society or world? By answering those two questions, you will ultimately come up with topics that are important to you and your fellow citizens. Many orations either discuss societal

issues or address personal issues that may plague our personal or professional lives. The best topics are ones chosen by students, not ones chosen by former orators or even coaches. If you believe in your topic, you can make it work. If you do not believe in the topic, you may fail to communicate any level of importance to the audience.

5. **After brainstorming,** research your top two or three topics. Can you find examples or stories to illustrate your ideas? Are there some interesting quotations that will spice up the topic? Although you should not rely on too much research, it is important for the success of your speech to have interesting supporting material. Common topics demand updated information to create interest for the audience.

6. **Do not change topics frequently.** A winning speech takes revision after each contest. Just because you do not receive "ones" is not a reason to abandon ship. Give your speech a reasonable amount of time before starting over. Often times, improvements in the introduction, research, and organization can significantly improve the audience's perception of a speech. Many students think that the first draft is very close to perfection. That is an incorrect assumption. Professional speech writers revise their work many times before a speech is actually presented.

Ultimately, topic selection involves your unique approach to the topic. Listen, read, and observe the world around you. Listen also to your heart. The topic will come to you and will give you satisfaction and success.

HOW ARE PEOPLE PERSUADED?

Any professional speaker will tell you there is an art to persuasion. The most important aspect of persuasion is a solid understanding of how people are persuaded? If you persuade them, they will vote for you. A good speech that makes no attempt at reaching the audience's feelings and thoughts does not work well.

Aristotle, recognized as the foremost authority in communication, explains that audiences are persuaded by three elements; **pathos, ethos,** and **logos.** With pathos, the speaker considers the needs, wants, and desires of the listeners. In other words the speaker tries to satisfy the listener with something that he or she inherently desires. With ethos, the audience evaluates the character of the speaker. Is the speaker credible enough to believe? Is the speaker confident and poised? Are the facts solid and presented with noble intentions? Is the speaker's appearance positive? Finally, logos is the logical side of the listeners. Is the speaker appealing to common sense and solid reasoning? Without logic, no amount of emotion nor a new dress or suit, will sway the judge. Aristotle believed that all three were quite important in the communication process.

When deciding on the best approach to a speech, you must do a great deal of **audience analysis**. Just as a salesclerk will fail to get the product sold if the wrong approach is used, so too will the orator fail to earn the acceptance of the audience without the right approach. Most competitive speeches have a combination of approaches that contribute to their success. They are not based solely on facts and statistics. They are not all based on emotional appeals. They are not all serious. They are not all humorous. A good speech combines several approaches to reach all types of judges.

Lanny Naegelin, coach at San Antonio Churchill High School, presents some very interesting research on what judges prefer, in his informative video tape "The Art of Oratory." Four distinct listener/learning styles are explained.

1. **Abstract random**
2. **Abstract sequential**
3. **Concrete sequential**
4. **Concrete random**

Many judges fall into one or more of these categories. The **abstract random** (#1) is a people person and is concerned with feelings. The **abstract sequential** (#2) prefers the rational; fosters intellect; looks for organization; demands statistics and substantive content. The **concrete sequential** (#3) is a hands on person who is very practical. Will solutions really work? The **concrete random** (#4) makes intuitive leaps and likes open possibilities. What if? What does it mean in the long term?

Mr. Naegelin points out how judges fit into these four areas of preference. He stresses the importance of writing the speech by appealing to all learning preferences. How is this done? A #1 prefers content based on humor, stories, personal examples, and involvement. A #2 prefers facts and statistics, expert opinion, logical order, and exact language. A #3 wants practical analysis and application, solid solutions, and tight organization. A #4 prefers effects, ramifications, illustrations (humorous or serious).

Mr. Naegelin points out how judges even differ on delivery techniques. With physical delivery, a #1 prefers personal warmth, good eye contact, relaxed conversational delivery. A #2 prefers gestures and movement that support meaning, clear articulation, and exact pronunciation. A #3 wants movement with a clear purpose. A #4 prefers unique elements of delivery style, open delivery with high energy.

Don't lose sleep over trying to aim at all types of listeners. Just do your best to reach and understand the diversity found in the learning styles and preferences of your audience. When you receive a wide variance in scores as competitors often receive in any forensics event, it is often because of audiences likes and dislikes. By addressing the emotional and logical sides of the listeners, you can appeal to and win the acceptance of your speech audience.

DEVELOPING THE SPEECH

ORGANIZING THE BODY

Once you select a solid topic and analyze the impact the topic might possibly have on your judges, you are ready to begin writing the rough draft of your speech. Before you actually begin writing, you should develop a comprehensive outline. This allows you to have a definite idea about the direction of the speech. Without an outline, you will probably spend more time making revisions with your script. I recommend writing just the body of the outline first. What main points do you want to make? What supporting details do you want to incorporate? The body is the heart of the speech and you should have a clear idea of what it is you want your audience to get out of the speech. After the main points are developed, give some thought to the introduction and the conclusion. If you can not immediately decide about the introduction or conclusion, go ahead and start writing the body of the speech. After you write the body of the speech, you will have a better idea as to what type of introduction will be effective and how to conclude the speech.

Indeed, the biggest decision you will make about the development of the body is the method of organization. The structure you choose will depend on the topic you have chosen. There are many **organizational patterns**. We will now discuss the two most popular patterns.

PROBLEM-SOLUTION

Many speakers in oratory utilize this simple, organizational structure. The speaker places most of the emphasis on describing the problem that he or she is explaining. The problem may be examined in terms of facts and statistics, the impact of this problem on our society, and the impact of the problem on individuals. Examples and stories are necessary to exemplify the problem and to provide a realistic discussion of the problem. An optional step, again depending on the topic, is the determination of the cause or causes of the problem. The extensive examination of the topic on several levels of thought is then followed by specific solutions. Most judges expect solutions. If the orator only develops a problem, the audience is left with a sense of futility. Without possible solutions the audience may walk away with an awareness of an issue, but will not know what can be or what should be done to remedy the problem. Solutions can be suggested on many levels. What can society do about the problem? This may be examined on a local, state, and national level. What can members of the audience do to change or alter the impact of this problem? Problem-solution is an effective way to build the body of an oration.

THE MOTIVATED SEQUENCE

Another effective method of organization is the motivated sequence. The conceptualization of this method originates from Purdue University Professor, Allan Monroe. Monroe developed a method of organization that combines problem-solution with steps to heighten motivation. The sequence of this approach is viewed in the following five steps.

I. The Attention Step

    A. The introduction should focus on getting attention and explaining the purpose.

II. The Need Step

    A. The main idea of the speech should be explained. A specific statement of the problem and the extent of the problem should be stated.

    B. A preview of the main aspects of the problem area should be sign posted.

C. The first main point is discussed. It may analyze the nature and extent of the problem.

D. The second main point is discussed. It may focus on another impact of the problem.

E. The third main point is revealed. It may discuss yet another impact of the problem or examine possible causes.

III. The Satisfaction Step

A. The speaker explains how the solutions remedy the problem in a satisfactory way.

IV. The Visualization Step

A. The speaker explains the benefits of the solution. A personal application of the solution is provided.

B. The speaker also explains the consequences of not adopting the solutions.

V. The Action Step

A. A final appeal is presented for the listener detailing what action he or she can take.

The motivated sequence then is an effective way of not only convincing your audience of a problem, but also motivating them to take specific action. The audience realizes that your topic is not just another speech, but rather a problem that can and must be solved. It is a very practical approach that is effective in oratory rounds and for speeches in the real world.

Either of these approaches works well as an organizational pattern. Talk with your coach after you write the outline and get some feedback about the pattern of organization you have selected. If your oration is not organized, it will not have the desired impact upon the judge. Many judges spend too much time trying to figure out what ideas are being expressed in original oratory. If that happens, you can not expect a positive reaction. A speech should never put the members of the audience into a guessing game mode. Judges do not want to spend time deciphering the message. Persuasion comes with clarity of purpose.

After you complete your outline, make sure you carefully assemble your research. What direct quotations do you want to use? What facts, statistics, and personal examples do you want to describe? Make sure you know exactly where to apply your research before you write the rough draft. With the body of the outline and the research in place, start the first draft.

A national qualifier in oratory wrote a problem-solution oration against the practice of censorship. After researching the topic and writing an outline, Kathy composed her rough draft. She was able to articulate exactly what she wanted to say and actually made only minor changes throughout the season.

Although many orators tend to share parts of their speech as they develop it, it is sometimes better to examine the rough draft when it is completed. At that point more valid criticisms and suggestions can be made. It's important to see the big picture. A double-spaced typed copy is preferable. A rough draft should not look too rough! With the draft on the computer, corrections will be easy to make.

INTRODUCTIONS AND CONCLUSIONS

THE KEY TO CREATING INTEREST AND LASTING IMPACT

Once the body is written, it is time to go back to the beginning for a carefully planned introduction. Your first task is to decide how to get the attention of the judge. One can not just announce the topic and proceed to the body of the speech. Obviously, Kathy didn't begin her speech on censorship by saying, "Today I will give my views on censorship." That only explains the subject and doesn't pull the judge into the speech. Instead, Kathy began by stating, "From now on, I am going to censor everything you read, watch, and write. After all, don't I know what is best for you?" It succeeded in getting the judge's attention. After that opening she clearly explained what censorship was and what her stand on the issue was going to be throughout the speech. The effective opening succeeded in capturing the attention of the audience and motivating them to want to listen to her views on censorship.

Another interesting introduction was provided by a young man whose speech title was "The Truth about Hollywood." He began by saying, "When I was a child, I starred in several television series and did many commercials. But now, I am a just a normal high school student like the rest of you in this room." He went on to introduce his topic which was about lying. He soon returned to his Hollywood story and began to discuss more details about his experience. With this young man's good looks, the audience totally believed that he was a childhood actor. It wasn't until later in the speech that the audience sensed that something was peculiar about his introduction. He returned to his opening, as orators often do in the conclusion. He concluded, " The truth about Hollywood is that I have never been there." He had successfully used his title, his attention getter, and his conclusion to get the number one ranking in this round. By the way, he made some great points about the dangers of lying. But you see, his introduction made this speech work. The topic was very good but the introduction and conclusion were great! He succeeded in creating and sustaining interest; while leaving a **lasting impact** long after the speech was delivered.

You don't have to have a gimmick like this young man, but you do have to use your imagination in order to think of a way to draw in the audience. Another type of introduction involves telling a story. The story can be real or hypothetical. If your topic is on day care abuse, you might begin by **telling a story** of a child that was victimized. You will capture the attention of your judge if you begin with a dramatic story that illustrates your topic. For beginning speakers, a good story works well with the audience. A story can be visualized and remembered far longer than mere facts and statistics about the problem. Another nice aspect of beginning with a story is that you can return to it at the end of the speech. With the day care abuse topic, it could be concluded by saying, "If we work to solve this crisis, kids like Susie, who I referred to in my introduction, will be spared of physical and mental abuse. They will get a chance to have a happy childhood like most of us experience." This is really a simple approach, but it works well with many members of the audience, especially community judges.

Another approach that can work well is the **personal** opening. Do not use this type of introduction unless the topic means a great deal to you. Many years ago, a young man opened his speech with a story of young boy named Sam who was not allowed to see his father because of a divorce settlement. It was a very powerful story. At the end of his speech, the orator concluded, " I know very well how hard it can be not to see your father. Because I'm Sam." The audience all had to hold back tears. It was a moving speech that deeply affected the audience because of the personal connection. The young orator who had just competed unsuccessfully in his first tournament, turned and said, " Now I know what they are looking for, and do I have a story to tell!" He came in on Monday with a long handwritten speech. He looked like he had not slept all weekend. Mike had a troubled past involving the use of drugs and a nightmarish journey through the juvenile justice system. His mother had died when he was young and his father had remarried shortly thereafter. It seemed to be the cause of his criminal pathway. Mike entered the next tournament with his new speech. Both Sam and Mike broke to finals. Mike used the same format as Sam, telling the story of his life, but not disclosing the fact that it was his story until the end of his speech. Mike finished 2nd and Sam finished third. Both young men made the NFL district final round that year. Both had used personal stories to enhance topics they fully understood. The content in the body for both speeches was outstanding. But the introduction and conclusion had significant impact on many of the judges.

Another young lady named Shawn, who liked debate much more than individual events, was going through much agony over the selection of her oration topic. After three weeks of indecision, she talked to her coach. Her coach was aware that her father had multiple sclerosis and it was affecting her school performance. She was dealing with so much at home by her dad's sudden inability to do the things he once did. The coach encouraged Shawn to write an oration about the problems facing handicapped people in this country. At first, she really didn't want to write the speech. She was simply too upset to discuss it. But after she got started, it quickly became therapeutic for her. Here was the toughest thing she had ever faced and she realized she could get it out in the open by writing a speech about it. She too described personal experiences her Dad had faced by being handicapped. She described an experience at a restaurant whereby a man in a wheelchair had great difficulty in using the rest room because there was not enough space between the tables to get there. Another story involved a mother telling her child not to get close to that man in the wheelchair as if he had a contagious disease. Through his experience, she established a clear need for education about handicapped people and a need for reform in handicapped accessibility. She revealed the fact that she had talked about her father in all of her examples, in the conclusion of her speech.

Shawn's original speech earned her trip to nationals. With the support of her father, she began giving this oration at handicapped organizations in our home town. In short, this speech was not only therapeutic for Shawn, but it helped her entire family deal with the crisis. No one was any happier about her qualification for nationals than her dad. She awarded the plaque to her dad. By the way, the same young lady was the top debate speaker at nationals during her next season. Her oratory speech motivated her to succeed in forensics activities. That success continued in college where she has earned a bachelor and master's degree with a 4.0 GPA and is now headed for law school. Oratory is an important event. It can have a great power over the speaker and society.

Other forms of attention-getters include poems, quotations from experts or famous people, shocking or startling the audience, a humorous anecdote, or a cartoon from a newspaper or magazine. The key is finding an approach that works well with your topic.

Realize that the way you begin and end your speech is very important to the success of your speech. Judges tend to remember those with clever introductions and conclusions. Use your imagination to come up with other original approaches.

It is also important that one does not just use an attention device in the intro as the entire intro. Many beginning speakers come up with a good story or quote and move directly to the body of the speech. An orator must explain the **thesis statement** of the speech. You must tell the judge exactly what you will be discussing. This may involve defining your topic, explaining why the judge should listen to this particular speech, or why you chose this topic. Many judges also prefer that the main points be previewed in the introduction. Check with your coach on the body preview. Some prefer that you let the main points unfold through the progression of the body. Clearly though, the introduction should prepare the listener for what he or she is about to hear.

The **conclusion** should summarize the speech content in terms of its importance to the world and appeal to the judge for change. The clincher can either connect the opening as in previous examples or conclude with a new quote or story. Without an imaginative introduction and a convincing conclusion, success may be limited. You will be judged on organization and that depends on the introduction, the body, and the conclusion. The judge expects you to develop all three areas well. Once you learn to construct the introduction, the body, and the conclusion, you will possess the foundation of speech writing. To be sure, if the judge is not clear on the relationship between the intro, the body, and the conclusion, your chances for success are greatly diminished. You will grow tired of reading about it on ballot after ballot. Get off to a good start with an organized speech and you will experience less frustration and more success.

TECHNIQUES OF DELIVERY

THE PRESENTATION

Because orations are written with passion, they should also be presented in a passionate manner. A well-written, moving speech presented in a robotic manner will fall short of fulfilling the orations's potential. Beginning orators especially have difficulty in communicating an oratory speech with the proper feeling. Clearly, a judge is not judging on the written speech. In fact, he or she will not see a copy of your speech. It must be conveyed through a single presentation. That is the fundamental difference between oral and written speech.

Many speakers fail to understand other key differences between oral and written language. In a formal essay, you never use contractions such as "can't" or "won't". However, in every day speech, we use contractions all the time. Likewise, they can be used in an oration for personal impact.

Some words that are very technical and formal, may come off as impersonal and lacking in impact. The same words in an essay would be regarded as impressive. In oratory you should consider the sound of the language. The rules of written language do not apply equally to speech writing. The sound of the language determines the degree of the success with your oration. Hence, the language used in the script should enable you to present the speech in a communicative manner.

One characteristic that is paramount to success in original oratory is **enthusiasm**. Enthusiasm involves having a strong desire to communicate with the audience. A judge should be able to spot enthusiasm both in your attitude towards your performance and in the way that you present the speech. Most successful orators and professional public speakers have a lot of enthusiasm. The audience can see it in their eyes and hear it in the use of their voice. Enthusiasm is often manifested with pure energy. The speaker displays energy, not lifelessness in the performance. Show your judge that you care about this topic and your performance. It will say a great deal about you and your attitude towards your presentation.

Sincerity is another derivative of enthusiasm that is important. In a debate round, the judge usually realizes that you are not overly sincere about your arguments since you have to debate both sides of the topic. While some speakers may pick a topic just to please judges, the more competitive orators pick topics they value internally and genuinely care about. They are sincere about the message they are communicating. Because many orators are not great actors, sincerity is easily discernible in a speech. It is difficult to convince a judge of your viewpoint with a topic that you yourself question. It is also important to maintain that sincerity in each oratorical presentation. If orators lose the sincerity and the positive enthusiasm, they will simply not receive an enthusiastic response from the audience.

Timing is very important in the delivery. While extemp speeches go along at a fairly consistent rate, oratory speakers display a strong sense of planned changes in the timing. Generally, an oration is presented in a slower, more deliberate manner. Oratory often possesses a dramatic quality. Remember, the judge has to be moved by the presentation. Orators often mark their script for pauses and underline important phrases they want to emphasize. There are times to speed up, especially on the lighter or humorous parts of the speech. There are times to slow down, especially on the more touching or emotional parts. In a memorized presentation, timing must be planned and is important to the overall success of the delivery.

The **physical aspects** of delivery are also important. An orator must appear relaxed with the stance. Hands should be at the sides of the body during the presentation. **Gestures** should be forceful at times when making an important argument or point. Speakers should reach out with open palms visible when appealing to the audience for change or acceptance. Gestures should be natural and used only when making key points. Never overuse gestures. They become distracting and defeat the purpose of using gestures in the first place. A gesture enhances and reinforces what is being verbalized. It does not take away from the message. Your coach will watch your practice speeches and give you advice on the effectiveness of your gestures. They are a critical aspect of your delivery. It will take time to develop the gestures that will work for you. Be patient with yourself as you work on the physical characteristics of delivery.

Movement is also necessary. Never stand in one spot for the whole ten minutes. It can make the entire presentation stagnant in the eyes of the audience. After your introduction, move to a new place. It might be a step or two to the left or right. Move again as you make a transition to a new point. It can be viewed as a visual transition for the audience. As you move from one point to the next, so does your body. In other words movement is a way to support speech transitions. Movement is also an excellent way to connect with members of the audience. One caution however, do not pace like television attorneys. That becomes very dis-

tracting. Nervous movement takes away from the presentation. Actors learn that movement has to be motivated. Speakers must learn the same principle. Ultimately, movement must seem spontaneous. One should not appear stiff and rigid in attempting to add movement to the presentation. The natural, spontaneous movement will make you and your audience comfortable with the delivery of your speech.

If possible, watch a final round of oration or ask your coach if he or she has any tapes of orators. It will help you visualize proper delivery techniques. Watch speeches on television. Watch speakers at church or at local city meetings. As in any other skill, the best way to learn is to observe others that possess strong skills. From careful observation, you will discover delivery characteristics that will improve your style of communication.

MEMORIZATION AND REHEARSAL

Memorization is not as difficult as it may appear. Many students say," I'm not good at memorizing. I could never learn an oration!" I have never had a student that could not memorize a speech. First, realize that your judge will not have a copy of the script. Only you will know if you make a mistake. It is often how you handle the mistake that makes the difference. If you make it painfully obvious, panicking or even admitting that you can not remember the words, it may be held against you. Try to recover quickly and continue the speech, getting as close to the wording as possible. But this will not even happen if you practice. Read the speech over to yourself several times. Learn it paragraph by paragraph. Practice in different settings. Rehearse in the car, at school , or even in the shower. When you get it down, practice in front of someone like your mom or dad or your best friend on the team. Then try it front of your coach. This scares my students. They usually mess up a bit and say," I really know this coach." I always say," I know you do. Your just nervous." After you can say it well for your coach, try presenting it to the whole class. Once that is mastered, you are ready to take it to the tournament and you will remember your speech. I promise!

Rehearsal is also important even after you have it learned. Without continuing to rehearse, you may forget it. Even when it gets a bit boring, rehearse so that your performance does not suffer. By using audio tape to evaluate the rate of your delivery, you can recognize if you are going too fast. Use a video tape to evaluate your physical delivery techniques. Your stance, gestures, and movement can be improved by watching yourself on a videotape. Many competitive orators rehearse before each round at tournaments. You really can not over rehearse. Just remember, each performance is new to the audience. Do not show that you are bored with the speech. You must get into it during each and every performance. After a sound schedule of rehearsals, you are now ready for the most exhilarating part of speech competition; the presentation of your original oratory speech at tournaments.

Good luck!

REVIEW

TOP NINE TIPS FOR SUCCESS IN ORATORY

1. Develop A Thorough Understanding Of The Potential Possibilities Of The Oratory Speech.

2. Select A Topic That Is Meaningful To You. Also Brainstorm As Many Topics As Possible And Research The Better Choices Before You Finalize Your Decision.

3. After Thoroughly Researching Your Topic, Write An Outline Of The Body Of Your Speech. Make It As Complete As Possible.

4. Develop A Creative Strategy For The Introduction And Conclusion.

5. Write The Rough Draft Following The Order Of Ideas In Your Outline.

6. As You Compose, Try To Use The Most Precise, Descriptive Language Possible To Accurately Express Your Viewpoint.

7. Submit A Typed Copy To Your Coach For Comments. After Making Revisions That Satisfy Your Coach, Memorize The Script.

8. Study Elements Of Effective Delivery.

9. Practice, Practice, Practice.

ACTIVITIES

1. Brainstorm for topics. Break up into small groups. Each group should come up with a least 20 topics. Have each group focus on a type of oratory. Choose mine or make up your own categories. Areas might include: values, pet peeves, societal problems, international issues, morality, pro-con issues. As a group, decide which topics might work best with judges. Look at the advantages and disadvantages of each topic. Have each person pick their favorite topic from the list. After five minutes, each person should give an impromptu speech on that topic. The group can then decide which topics are convincing and worth pursuing.

2. Play devil's advocate. For each controversial impromptu speech, have a person give a counter position. Which side is most convincing? Forget about your personal opinions. Be open-minded.

3. Finally, practice the art of persuasion through real life situations. Role play giving a speech in the following situations.

   a. You are two hours past curfew. Explain to your parents why you are late and convince them that you shouldn't be grounded.

   b. You have been accused of plagiarism of a term paper in English. Prove the authenticity of your writing to the teacher.

   c. You have accidentally scratched the family car. Explain what happened getting your parents to sympathize with you rather than to get mad at you for the accident.

4. Take a topic that you know well and write a sample outline using either the problem–solution organizational pattern or the Monroe method. You may want to try both just to compare the two methods. Show your outline to group members for suggestions. Hand it in to your forensics coach.

The following list of topics were chosen through brainstorming with my forensics class. Some were taken from national and state tournaments. Again, choose a topic that you feel strongly about and one that judges may accept. These topics are offered just to give you a concept of what can be chosen as topics in original oratory.

Guilt	Teen pregnancy
Extremism	A need for volunteers
Procrastination	The two party political system
Heroes	Motivation
Education	Respect
Medical ethics	Boredom
Taking risks	Creativity
Laughter	Political term limits
Suicide	Vouchers for schools
Societal violence	The pace of contemporary life
Media manipulation	Frivolous law suits
Greed	Competition
Lack of honor	Morals
Animal experimentation	Nutrition and health
Political action committees	A sports minded society
Organ donation	Divorce
Homelessness	Children of divorce
Rape	America: united we stand, divided we fall
Ethics for journalists	
Capital punishment	Planting trees
Censorship	Teen alcoholism
Computer crime	Drugs and youth
Welfare	Apathy
Handicapped discrimination	Cultural diversity
Domestic abuse	Buck passing
Gun control	The importance of our name
Ebonics	Progress
Missing children	Maintaining hope
Affirmative action	Concentration
Protection of the environment	Imagination
Drunk driving	Aids
Euthanasia	The global perspective
Immigration	Hate groups
Diplomatic immunity	Child abuse
Goal setting	Cults and mass suicide
Drug laws	

CHAPTER 3

Extemporaneous Speaking

After completing this chapter you should be able to:

❏ Define extemporaneous speaking

❏ Realize the benefits of extemporaneous speaking

❏ Prepare an extemp file

❏ Know where to find information for extemp speeches

❏ Know and use methods of organizing an extemp

❏ Use effective techniques of extemporaneous speaking

❏ Answer an extemp question

New Terms To Learn In This Chapter

Extemporaneous

Extemp Preparation

Organizational Patterns

Source Cites

AN INTRODUCTION TO EXTEMPORANEOUS SPEAKING

Throughout your life there will be many situations requiring the ability to quickly analyze issues and subsequently discuss them. It may be an oral response to a teacher's question or an oral response to a customer's complaint at work. The skills required for effectively communicating in situations involving limited preparation and fluent delivery are learned and exercised in **extemporaneous** speaking.

In extemporaneous speaking you study current events and draw questions on the issues. You are given thirty minutes to prepare a speech answering a question. The process is repeated for each round of competition. Extemporaneous speaking is comparable to the job of broadcast journalism. Journalists must report facts about current events and help shape public opinion on these issues. Extemporaneous speakers function much like professional news analysts.

Many students initially shy away from extemporaneous speaking because of the brief preparation time. They often say, "That sounds hard!" But if students didn't want to be challenged, they would not pursue individual events in the first place. Extemporaneous speaking is not really all that difficult. In fact many extempers feel that it is easier, year after year, than other speech events requiring memorization. The stress over finding the right topic is absent. And the fact that a new topic is discussed each round makes it far less boring. Extemporaneous speaking then has unique challenges and advantages over other speech events.

WHY PARTICIPATE IN EXTEMPORANEOUS SPEAKING?

Let's face it. Most speaking situations in your life will come closer to extemporaneous speaking than any other form of communication. Consider the classroom. Your history teacher asks you a question in class about the causes of the Civil War. You read about it the night before in the assigned reading. The question demands that you articulate an oral response by recalling the reading assignment and analyze the key points of the reading. There are simply many classroom experiences whereby you are asked to analyze an issue or fact. Those that did not read the assignment will engage in impromptu speaking. An impromptu response is one in which a person has little preparation time before speaking. Extemporaneous speaking presents a more reasonable challenge because you study the subject before discussing it.

In our **personal lives** we are often asked to share opinions on issues both locally and nationally. Those responses are given over the phone or in person. Such experiences require us to synthesize what we know and articulate an immediate response. These situations are quite easy for those who have participated in extemp and often difficult for the average person without extemp experience.

At **work** bosses often want oral reports on an aspect of the business. In preparing such a speech, you would not be successful if the report was written word for word and read in that fashion. By writing out the report, the employee demonstrates a lack of confidence in his or her ability to explain the business orally. It would also sound boring and even sound childish if it were read word for word. A solid report should be presented like an extemp speech. You should demonstrate your knowledge in an organized manner.and display effective communication skills. Both skills are learned in extemp speaking.

Extemporaneous speaking can be found somewhere in the middle of a continuum between a very limited preparation situation such as impromptu, and memorized presentations such as oratory. Indeed, it is the essence of most practical speaking situations in our personal and professional lives.

THE BENEFITS OF PARTICIPATION IN EXTEMPORANEOUS SPEAKING

Any former extemporaneous competitor will agree that extemporaneous speaking is one of the most **educational activities** in school. In extemp students become familiar with issues and concerns that many either do not want to learn about or are not taught about in school. Very few people have a real interest in current events before participating in extemp. With the exception of the sensationalized stories or events of great magnitude like war, most of us choose not to become informed about the issues that affect our well-being. It is easy to be bored with issues such as homelessness, economic trends, or politics. As an extemper you will gradually become interested in these issues. A former extemporaneous speaker, now a successful aerospace engineer in a major aircraft company, indicated that he misses reading magazines for extemp and now feels somewhat out of touch with what is really going on in the world. He believes extemp forced him to come to grips with the issues of the world. He said also that his ability to give an extemp speech was invaluable in his college classes and in his job expectations.

In one sense an extemper plays the role of news analyst. The extemper has to first understand what is going on in the news and then proceed to offer analysis of the news. Jane Pauley, the highly successful broadcast journalist, claimed that her participation in extemporaneous speaking prepared her more for the job she has today than anything else she studied in high school. Ms. Pauley made an impressive showing in extemp at the national tournament when she was in high school.

Many people have opinions about issues but fail to read much about those issues. Therefore, their opinions are based on intuition and not facts. Moreover, some citizens vote for leaders without really understanding the issues the politicians are discussing. Extempers are **informed citizens** and will not be misled by empty rhetoric and misinformation.

Another advantage is that extemp significantly **improves speech fluency**. While many people are hesitant when speaking about an issue, extempers display a consistent fluency. They learn to speak without hesitation and are able to communicate clearly and persuasively to their audience. I once had a teacher come into my classroom after school. She observed one of my senior extempers explaining some concepts to an eager novice. After a few minutes, she asked, "What department does she teach in?" I replied, "Oh she is one of our extemporaneous speakers. She is a senior." My colleague could not believe it. How a high school student could speak with such fluency and knowledge amazed this teacher. By the way that extemper is now practicing law in a major law firm in the United States. There is something about participation in extemp that develops fluency in public speaking like no other event.

Debaters can improve their fluency by participating in extemp. Clearly, the toughest aspect of debate speaking is developing fluency. You are presented a case in outline form and have just a few minutes to refute the points of that case. Debaters who also extemp develop fluency much faster than those who do not participate in extemp. Two former students that placed in the top ten for debate speakers at nationals also qualified in extemp for nationals. Extemp gave them the skills in fluency that enabled them to become successful communicators in debate.

Extempers also become **great researchers**. By becoming familiar with the best magazines, you learn much about the nature of research and what can or can not be found in certain publications. While some students grudgingly tackle research projects and papers, extempers proceed with ease at such assignments. Extemp enables one to research quickly and accurately.

As you can see, there is much to learn from participation in extemporaneous speaking and little to lose. Extemp will simply bring out qualities in you that you may or may not have known you had. Just ask your coach about it. He or she will affirm the fact that extemp will help you in many ways. Moreover, the skills you develop will enhance your success in whatever career pathway you choose in life.

EXTEMP IN A NUTSHELL

Before we get to the specifics of preparation, let's examine what takes place in the process of **extemporaneous preparation**. Read articles from some of the major news magazines and file them under categories such as domestic issues and foreign affairs. With the help of your extemp colleagues, you will develop a body of information on most of the major stories in the news. You need to read the articles carefully before attending your first tournament. Your file will be used in the extemp prep room at the tournaments that your squad attends. At an assigned time you will draw three questions. You will select the best topic for your extemp speech. At that point , you will have thirty minutes to write your speech outline. The first step will be to pull articles on your topic from your file. After quickly reviewing your information, you will begin writing the body of your speech outline. Generally, you will pick two or three main points that must be explained in answering your question. Then, you will decide upon the most appropriate introduction and conclusion. At this point you will have about enough time to practice your extemp speech prior to presenting it to your judge. This process is repeated for each round of extemporaneous speaking.

PATIENCE: A NECESSARY VIRTUE

Few important things in life are learned overnight. Students of extemp must be patient. Few individuals give a good extemp speech, right off the bat. It takes practice. Like anything else, do not adopt a "I can't do it attitude." You would have never learned math, science, or foreign language without some patience and perseverance. Similarly, you will soon become

comfortable with the process of extemporaneous speaking. It is the repetition that will allow you to learn how to give an extemp speech. And it will not take that long. With a little patience you will soon be giving solid extemp speeches and you will feel proud of your accomplishment. *You can do it!*

EXTEMP PREPARATION

Extempers must have a well developed file to be prepared to speak. Coaches occasionally allow a few young teams to carry a box of magazines to tournaments. The novice extempers attempt to write a topical index identifying what articles are in certain magazines. Failure is imminent with such a system. First, the index becomes too lengthy. Next, magazines soon disappear after tournaments and practices. With a thirty minute prep time, you simply do not have enough time to depend on such an inefficient system of organization.

Most extempers carry a **cut file**. This box or crate has file folders clearly labeled on all important aspects of current events. The National Forensic League divides extemporaneous speaking into two separate events. They are United States extemp and foreign extemp. Depending on your state and the size of the tournaments, you may have combined extemp which allows you draw questions from your area of preference or requires you to choose from both areas. Here are some sample categories from a recent national tournament to give you an idea of the general categories you might use for filing.

United States extemp:

- U.S. Trade Policy
- President Clinton and the 105th Congress
- Economic Growth and the 21st Century
- Law, Courts, and Crime
- Welfare and Social Issues
- The American Condition — Virtues, Values, and Ethics
- Arts and Entertainment

- People in the News
- Political Scandals
- The Political Parties and the National Legislature
- The State of the State
- Public Affairs
- Public Service
- Science, Technology, and the Environment
- Education and Issues of America's Youth

Foreign extemp:

- Africa
- Russia the Eurasian Republics
- Western Europe
- Middle East
- Asian Sub-Continent
- Mexico, The Caribbean Islands, and Central America
- South America

- The Polar Regions
- Worldwide Environmental Issues
- International Social Issues
- China and the Pacific Rim
- International Organizations
- International Terrorism
- Diplomacy
- U.S. Foreign Policy

Of course, topics change from year to year, depending on domestic issues and worldwide trouble spots. Start with your own areas and then expand as your research progresses.

Computerized file systems can also be very significant in the search for information. File card programs are available for many computers, including lap tops. The computers may not be used at most tournaments for the retrieval of information. But they may be invaluable for setting up your file.

HOW TO BEGIN AND MAINTAIN AN EXTEMP FILE

A PRACTICAL METHOD OF FILING

Mr. Joseph Johnson, coach at Madison High School in San Antonio, has developed a practical method of extemp filing. It is based on the need for quick and easy access to the information since time is critical in this activity. Also, the system is beneficial for novices so that they can become knowledgeable with the filing system in a short amount of time. A good extemper should not have to guess what the topics will be in the draw, they should be **prepared** for them. Here are some of the key elements of the system.

1. This system is based upon a categorizing method. It is broken down into categories that are commonly used in extemp competition. Each category is separated into topics. If the topics are broad, they are then divided into sub-topic areas.

   Example: Eu - England, Budget

   The category is Europe.
   The topic is England.
   The sub-topic is Budget.

2. It requires articles to be extracted from the magazines. The articles should be labeled with information that makes it easy to file. The date and name of the source should be placed at the bottom of the page. The article's category, topic, and sub-topic should be placed on the upper right side of the page. This will prevent the articles from being misfiled if it is separated from the file.

3. When you begin to set up the system you should alternate each file tab from left, middle, and right. This allows a team to add or take out a file without having tabs overlapping each other. Each file tab is labeled with a category, topic, and sub-topic. Colored labels for each category are used to visually separate the categories.

4. The catalog is the heart of the system. It allows novices to re-

search and file without crowding over the files. Traditionally, only experienced team members could create and maintain a file.

5. The filing system does not separate foreign division and domestic division. Extempers tend to be too limited on knowledge when they focus on their own division.

6. Cross referencing is much easier under this system.

Below is a sample from the catalogue of the Madison extemp file

E-	Economy		S	Social	
E-	Corporations	MNC's	S	Abortion	Pro Choice
E-	Corporations	Apple	S	Abortion	Pro Life
E-	Corporations	CEO'S	S	Child Abuse	
E-	Federal Reserve Board		S	Crime	Automobile Theft
E-	Industry, Airline		S	Drugs	Abuse
E-	Tax	Capital Gains	S	Education	
J	Judicial		I	International	
J	Abortion		I	APEC	
J	Affirmative Action		I	China	
J	Checks and Balances		I	Cuba/US Relations	
J	Constitutional amendments		I	Human Rights	
J	School prayer		I	Negotiations	Middle East
J	Supreme Court	Members	I	UN	Peacekeeping

As you can see, this is a concise method of categorizing your information for extemp. It is important that your squad either develops a workable method or adopts one similar to the preceding example.

Working together on a extemp file is preferable. It maximizes preparation time significantly. However, you must be knowledgeable about the articles in your file. Read as much as you can prior to the rounds. It will help you immensely!

WHERE TO FIND EXTEMP INFORMATION

Begin with the "big three" *magazines*. They are *Time, U.S. News and World Report,* and *Newsweek*. Beginning extempers will get an excellent overview of domestic and international issues in these three magazines. All three tend to focus on similar stories. Some beginners will get along fine just reading one of these weekly publications.

Now because most students have access to the "big three," competitive extempers must go beyond these sources. Other popular magazines include:

Business Week;	providing excellent economic outlooks for the business world.
Congressional Digest;	a pro-con look at controversial issues in government.
Current History;	depicting issues within regions of the world.
National Journal;	discusses new governmental issues.
National Review;	examines current issues.
The New Republic;	examines current issues from different perspectives.
World Press Review;	foreign press observations about our world.
The Economist;	depicting current economic trends and issues.
Forbes;	deals with a variety of contemporary issues.
Fortune;	Contemporary issues.
Foreign Policy;	international issues.
Foreign Affairs;	international issues.

There are many other publications. Go to your library or bookstore and browse.

Newspapers are also excellent sources for extemp files. Your local newspaper will carry many national and international stories. They may provide editorial commentary on many issues giving you good evidence for your speeches. Some popular national newspapers include **The Christian Science Monitor, The Wall Street Journal**, and **The New York Times**. Many extempers like using the **Christian Science Monitor** because of its easy to read format. The articles are often concise and to the point. Of course, **The Wall Street Journal** gives an update on economic trends. **The New York Times** covers all types of issues, domestically and internationally. Many libraries have NewsBank, an index to newspapers across the country. Extempers often find the NewsBank useful for coming up with original sources of information.

The **Internet** is also invaluable to the accessing of newspapers. Every major domestic and international newspaper can be found on the Internet. Their web cites also provide a concise summary of the major stories. This is useful for both novice and experienced extempers. Having Internet at home or at school will be advantageous to today's extemper. It is a faster and less expensive way to learn about current issues.

There are also excellent television programs that will develop your insight on the issues. Extempers should watch several national network and cable news programs each week. Many of the morning news shows are also helpful in learning about specific issues. There are also weekly news programs that are especially helpful in reflecting on the major news events of the preceding week. With stations that now focus on news exclusively, extempers can always find useful information on television. Popular programs are:

"Meet the Press;" a weekly news program interviewing important political figures.
"Inside politics;" a CNN look at the political scene.
"World Report ;" a CNN must- see for foreign extempers.
"Both Sides;" a CNN pro-con look at issues.
"Crossfire;" a CNN entertaining debate by political representatives of both parties.

Extempers can refer to news programs as source cites. However, you should make reference to a news program no more than once in a speech and that program should be televised within the last week. Even though most of your references should be in print, news programs will deepen your ability to analyze issues. Many of these television journalists cultivated their interest in current events with extemp. However, be cautious of the sensationalized newscasts. There is a big competitive market for viewers. Make sure you pick and choose your programs. The bottom line is that the more you know about the world, the more intelligent you will sound when you give your analysis of the extemp questions.

THE EXTEMP SPEECH

ANSWERING THE QUESTION

We have all watched politicians who, when asked a question by a citizen or a journalist, evade the question. There is a tendency for politicians to dance around the heart of a question. They either do not a have a grasp of the issue or do not want a negative reaction to their stance on the issue. Likewise, extempers must first and foremost answer the specific question. I have heard judges comment that many extempers do not answer the question. These judges admit that they are intelligent kids and good speakers, but simply fail to answer the question as written. Hence, the first rule to acknowledge about extemp is simple; *Answer the specific question as it is stated!*

It is also important to make a wise choice when selecting your question. Examine your three choices carefully. Choose the topic that you comprehend. Consider also whether it is a worthwhile topic for the audience. A great speaker with an unimportant question will not meet his potential in the extemp round. Of course a significant topic is important in any speech situation. There are weak topics that are written for invitational tournaments. Try to avoid them. Pick more substantive topics and your audience will be more receptive and better informed from your speech.

To answer the question, study it carefully. Do not panic and hurry into writing your outline until you are sure what is meant by the question. Always carry a pocket dictionary to look up any unfamiliar terms. Once you understand the implications of the question, you are ready to construct your speech.

Do not assume that your audience fully understands the underlying issue being discussed. At some point in your speech, either in the introduction or as supporting detail for a main point, background information is useful if the judge is to truly understand your analysis. This advice is particularly relevant in foreign issues, where the audience may lack a fundamental understanding of the problem. It is not as necessary with domestic issues, where the judge possesses some familiarity with the issue.

It is also important to answer the question in a clear and straightforward manner. Many questions demand a yes or a no response. Consider the question, "Should a balanced budget amendment be adopted by Congress?" It would be proper to answer the question in the introduction with a yes or a no. The main points would explain the basis for that yes or no response. There are some who fear that an immediate yes or no response may turn the judge against the extemper if the judge disagrees with the position. However, if solid reasons are given for the speaker's position, that will not be a factor in the judge's decision. The worst mistake many extempers make is keeping the judge in the dark, oscillating back and forth on the issue. The judge, meanwhile, is trying to understand just what the person is trying to convey. *A key aspect of extemp involves clarity.* If one loses the judge by evading the question, then little is really communicated. Like the debater who fails to explain his position and consequently loses the round, so too, can an extemper lose the judge through ambiguous rambling. Clarity of purpose in extemp can not be overemphasized.

Finally, pick topics that you understand; that you have some information on; and that have a general importance for you and our society. If you choose the most worthwhile topic, your response from the audience will be positive. After one of my young extempers received a rank of six out of six contestants, I asked the dejected speaker what question he had drawn. He responded, "Do Beavis and Butthead have social relevance to our society?" When I asked him about his other two choices, he retorted, "I didn't have a file on either of them. Besides, they were tough topics." When a judge hears a speech about Beavis and Butthead, not known for their speech eloquence by the way, he or she may be far more interested in a question about television censorship. Be smart when you pick your question. Don't select your topic on the basis of shock value or simplicity. The *choice of the question* is very important in the extemp process.

ORGANIZING THE EXTEMP SPEECH

THE INTRODUCTION

As in any forensics speech, the introduction is important in gaining the attention of the judge. Your introduction should consist of an attention getter, an exact statement of the question, your approach in answering the question, and a preview of main points. The introduction should take about one minute to a minute and fifteen seconds. I have listened to extemp introductions that were excessive in length. As a result the speaker failed to adequately answer the question and also had a weak conclusion. I would advise allowing sufficient time for the body and the conclusion.

There are many types of openings or **attention getters**. Because your judges, like many members of our society, may not be keenly interested in current events, you have to draw them into your topic. I have judged many young extempers that simply begin with their question. That's a big mistake. One must get the audience interested in the topic. A popular attention getter is an **analogy**. The extemper begins by telling a story that can be related to the question. If you get the judge to smile at your story, you have increased the likelihood that the judge will listen to the rest of your speech. The analogy can be a fable, a poem, or an anecdote. They can be found in poetry books, nursery rhymes, or magazines such as Reader's Digest. One example might be to use the poem "Casey at the Bat". Begin your speech by stating," In a well-known poem entitled "Casey at the Bat", the baseball team of Mudville relies on Casey, their star player to make that big hit in an important game. Casey swaggers up to the plate, fully confident, along with the rest of the crowd that he'll hit that home run. But Casey's overconfidence proves to be his downfall, and the mighty Casey strikes out." Then link the attention getter to the topic," Casey's quest for success is very similar to our President's attempt to hit a home run with the issue of gun violence." Relating a simple story can be an effective way to capture attention.

Another analogy used by a successful extemper revolved around a boy scout. It seems that a young boy scout arrived at his scout meeting with a black eye. When the scout master asked him what happened, he replied that he had tried to help an old lady across the street. "How in the world?" his scout master asked, "Could you get a black eye doing that?" To which the scout replied, "She didn't want to go." He then went on to compare the scout story to the President's effort to lead the people of the United States into a direction they didn't want to go. It was a humorous analogy that connected well to some questions.

It is important, however, that an analogy be used only when it truly fits the topic. To make an analogy fit every topic, is poor practice. Each topic requires a special attention getter that will fit the specific topic.

Another excellent approach is to use **political cartoons**. These are often about specific issues. Judges perhaps prefer this type of opening because of the humor and because they are so topic specific. Keep your eye open as you read your daily paper or any other paper or magazine. You may find some great extemp openings.

Other extempers do well with **famous quotations** found in almost any quotations book. It is easy to connect famous quotations to many topics. Many of them are organized by subject matter. Contemporary quotations are particularly effective.

Some extempers begin with some historical background of the topic. This can be especially solid for foreign issues whereby the judge may know little about past conflicts in an area of the world. This really can be effective and some may prefer this approach over a humorous one. It can also provide justification for the topic.

The bottom line is that it depends on the topic as to the method of getting the judge's attention. Don't use the same approach over and over. Adapt to the question that you draw. The best type of opening is **topic specific.** As you read sources of information, look for topic specific attention grabbers. Audiences will be most impressed when your opening is specifically relevant to the topic.

Step two in the intro involves connecting the attention getter to the question. I call it the link. Link the opening to the question area. Many students make the **link** by indicating that this opening is much like the

situation occurring in the world today. Often, background information on the issue is provided to establish not only the link, but to establish the importance of the question. They will then conclude the link step by stating, "That is why many Americans are asking the question, what can be done to curb homelessness in the United States?"

After an exact statement of the question, the extemper then previews the main points. He states; "Now to fully answer this question, we must address three main points or three areas of analysis. After stating those three points very concisely, the extemper concludes the introduction and moves to the body of the speech.

THE BODY

Organizing the body of the extemp speech is perhaps the most important part of the planning process. There are many different ways of organizing the body. The method one chooses is dependent upon the type of question one has drawn. One very popular method of organization is **unified analysis**. In unified analysis the body of the speech serves as a justification for that answer.[1] Many extempers dance around the heart of the question ignoring the intent of the question. With unified analysis, the answer to the question is stated first, and the speech serves to justify that answer. Often, the extemper provides much analysis and only answers the question in the conclusion of the speech. This only confuses the audience and creates ambiguity in the speaker's purpose. When an extemper states, "In answering the question, I will have three areas of analysis," they are not using unified analysis. According to proponents of unified analysis, if the information does not answer the question, then it does not belong in the speech.[2]

Before examining examples of unified analysis and other patterns of organization, it is important to review the types of extemp questions. These are: **questions of fact**, which ask for a description of an issue or a prediction of the outcome of an issue based on the facts of the matter; **questions of value**, which ask for an application of personal or societal norms to an issue, and **questions of policy**, which ask for an evaluation of a solution or a prescription for a solution to a problem.[3]

There are also two ways the questions are asked: closed questions and open questions. Closed questions ask for an unconditional affirmative or negative answer. The questions normally begin with "can" or "will." The answer is stated immediately after the question, and the major points in the speech are reasons supporting that answer. Open questions do not ask for a definitive answer. They allow for many possible approaches. Open questions often begin with "what" or "how."[4]

Here are two outlines of extemp speeches answering closed questions using unified analysis.

Question: "Is Japan now the most powerful nation in the world?"
Answer: No.
Thesis: Japan is not the most powerful nation in the world.
    I. Because it is economically isolated
        A. does not provide leadership in APEC
        B. does not forcefully advocate GATT

---

[1] "Organizing an Extemporaneous Speech Using Unified Analysis," Robert Carroll, *Rostrum*, April, 1995. And "An Introduction to Extemporaneous Speaking and Commentary," by Robert Carroll.
[2,3,4] Robert Carroll

II. Because it is politically weak
    A. reform struggles in Diet show internal weakness
    B. trade struggles show external weakness
        1. United States
        2. South Korea
        3. China

Question: "Should tighter controls be placed on political campaign spending?"
Answer: Yes.
Thesis: Tighter controls should be placed on political campaign spending.
    I. Because it would recruit better candidates
        A. candidates need to be personally wealthy
        B. candidates need not pander to special interests
    II. Because it would improve democracy
        A. candidates need to meet voters
        B. candidates need to provide substance

Here are two outlines of extemp speeches answering open questions using unified analysis.

Question: "How should Congress balance the federal budget?"
Answer: Increased revenues and decrease expenditures.
Thesis: Congress should balance the federal budget by increasing revenues and decreasing expenditures
    I. Increase revenues
        A. raise consumption taxes
        B. raise personal income taxes
    II. Decrease expenditures
        A. reduce entitlement spending
            1. Social Security
            2. Medicare
        B. reduce defense spending
            1. lack of Soviet threat
            2. need for smaller, more mobile force

Example: "How serious is the problem of urban decay?"
Answer: Very serious.
Thesis: The problem of urban decay is very serious.
    I. Decaying resources is a serious problem
        A. Deteriorating physical resources

       B. Deteriorating human resources
   II. Decaying quality of life is a serious problem
       A. Constant violent crime
       B. Widespread poverty[5]

As you can see, the unified analysis approach makes a great deal of sense. If the extemper's goal is to answer the question, then the speech should be organized to meet that objective.

There are other traditional methods of organization that are also useful to the extemper. Many questions ask the extemper to analyze the success of public policy to solve a particular problem. Such questions are questions of policy. With such topics, we need to consider:

Problem-Solution

Consider the topic; "What should be done to overhaul the welfare system in the United States?" This type of question can be organized successfully with the problem-solution format. A two part structure might include:

    A. Problems of the welfare system
    B. Solutions to reform welfare

A three part structure might include:

    A. Problems of the welfare system
    B. Current proposals of reform
    C. Best proposal we should choose

Since so many domestic topics involve societal or political problems, the problem-solution pattern is a very practical one to use. International issues also can be discussed with the problem-solution pattern. Another type of organizational pattern that is effective is:

The Pro-Con Organization

Consider the topic, "Is capital punishment a necessity in the American judicial system?" The pro-con method works well with such a topic. A two part structure might include:

---

[5] Robert Carroll

A. Advantages of capital punishment.
B. Disadvantages of capital punishment.

With the two part structure, the question would be answered in the conclusion. With the three part structure, the question would be answered in the C point.

A. Advantages of capital punishment
B. Disadvantages of capital punishment
C. The favored position

Since controversy abounds in extemp questions, the pro-con method of organization is highly effective. But objective treatment often requires a balanced look before picking a side. There are many times, however, that one may give a more convincing speech by simply giving three reasons defending one position on such issues. In this approach, the three main points are the arguments that defend the yes or no position.

There are also questions that demand a break down of the main topic into smaller sub- topics. This is called a:

A Topical Organization Pattern

Consider the question; "Is the United States clearly the superpower of the world?" A three part subdivision might include:

A. Military might
B. Economic status
C. World leadership role

Hence, we offer three characteristics of international status and analyze how the U.S. measures up in these areas.

Consider the question; "What can the United States do to ease the tensions between China and Taiwan?" A two part structure might include:

A. Initiate talks between the two countries
B. Establish foreign policy that equalizes U.S. treatment of both countries.

There are simply many topics in which one needs to subdivide the main topic into two or three sub-topics.

When one has a question that requires a comparison between the past and the present, it can be useful to use a chronological:

Chronological Organizational Pattern

Consider the question; "How has the United States changed its role as world leader since the end of the cold war?

A two part structure might include:

A. Our role during the cold war
B. Our role after the cold war

Many topics lend themselves to a breakdown of past, present, and future. Occasionally, one must look at different parts of the world or the United States in analyzing a topic. This can be called a:

Regional Organizational Pattern

Consider the question; "Can the Democrats regain control of Congress? One could look at a three part structure by discussing:

A. Their chances in the West
B. Their chances in the East
C. Their chances in the South

By discussing the party's chances in those regions of the country, one could effectively answer the question.

The bottom line on organization is that there is not one method. These are only some suggestions to get started. You need to experiment with what works best for you and the specific question you have chosen. However, the organizational pattern needs to enhance clarity. It must be a pattern that allows the judge to clearly see the justification for your answer to the extemp question.

THE CONCLUSION

Of the three parts of the extemp outline, the conclusion is neglected the most. Many judges feel that quite a few extempers fail to properly finish the speech. Often, the extemper spends too much time on the introduction or the body, failing to leave sufficient time to conclude. Since the conclusion is the last impression one makes with the judge, it is a mistake to overlook it. Many extempers simply feel that the repetition isn't needed. But a three part structure must have the third critical segment, the conclusion.

In the conclusion the extemper should provide an exact restatement of the question. It might be worded in the following manner. "Therefore, when we look at the question, What should be done to reduce the federal budget deficit?, we need to remember the key points of my speech. After the topic restatement, provide a summary explaining how you have answered the question. Go over the main points emphasizing the main ideas and perspectives on the question. This should take about 45 seconds. Then go back to your opening, analogy or quote, and connect it to the perspective you have developed in the speech.

In the "Casey at the Bat" analogy, you might conclude by saying, "Somewhere men are laughing, somewhere men will shout, there is no joy in Washington, the mighty President has struck out." Many extempers use their creativity to carefully connect the intro and the conclusion. Regardless of the type of attention getter, it is easy to return to it in the clincher of the speech for a fitting conclusion. Of course, we use a clincher so that the ending sounds good. Listen to television journalists. They never end a report with "That's it" or "That's all I have ". When extempers say "That's it," it almost invites a sarcastic response from the listener. If you end with a carefully worded conclusion utilizing a bit of wit, you will conclude successfully and create a positive and lasting impression on the judge.

ADVICE FOR EXTEMP PREP PERIOD

Don't panic! Many extempers let anxiety destroy their productivity in the prep period. If you do not like the topic, realize that you will have more rounds. Occasionally, you will speak on a topic that you are not familiar with or dislike. Be calm and begin work without fear or hesitation.

Quickly review your files on the topic. If you have read and highlighted your files, you should be able to extrapolate the key ideas quickly. You will need to use **source cites**. Extemp is like debate. The judge is not going to take your word on everything. Yes, you are providing the analysis, but you must refer to your sources for proof. This involves giving the name and date of the magazine or newspaper. Make a direct quote if possible or a close paraphrase. The quotes should be short. Many extempers make their source cites only a sentence or two in length. Beginning extempers should use at least one source cite for each main point or three for the body of the speech. As you get more experienced, you should try to incorporate additional source cites. Speakers should aim toward a minimum of five and not exceed ten. Also, try to quote from different sources. This proves to the judge that you are well read. It also proves that your perspective is based on more than one source and will make you appear more objective in your answer to the question. Many good extempers do a nice job presenting a fluent speech, but fail to provide any evidence to support their conclusions. Make source cites a priority. They give you credibility. However, do not fabricate source cites. It is unethical to make up your extemp quotes just like it would be unethical to make up debate quotes. Extempers also should not give source cites just for the sake of giving source cites. It is the quality of your references that will be impressive to the audience, not the quantity.

As discussed earlier, write the body of the speech first. Then go back and construct the introduction and the conclusion. Many extempers write their outline in bigger print on a legal pad. NFL contests do not allow any notes when delivering the speech to the judge. You may want to practice with notes to get the content down, although many extempers practice without notes. In either case, it is still necessary to write a speech outline. You also want to write down which points you will document with source cites.

Finally, allow enough time to **practice** your speech. Do not let the actual presentation be your only performance. That is very risky. Most competitive speakers practice before performing in front of the judge. Do not feel too inhibited to talk to a locker or a wall. That is all part of the game of forensics, and it is an integral part of the game.

DELIVERY TIPS

Don't rush through your speech. Many judges feel that extempers tend to talk too fast. Although the delivery is a bit faster than delivery used in oratory, it is still fairly slow especially compared to debating. If the speed is slower, your enunciation will be solid. Extempers, like news analysts, must communicate clearly.

Use **gestures** to emphasize important points in your speech. Do not over-gesture. Judges feel that many extempers repeat hand movements over and over. When this happens, the gestures become distracting and defeat the point of gestures. Likewise, an absence of gestures make you appear rigid and stiff. You also miss an important advantage of public speaking, the chance to use the body to add emphasis to the ideas you are communicating.

Standing in one place for seven minutes is boring. You should have motivated **movement**. After the introduction take a step or two to the left or right. After your first main point, take another step or series of steps. Repeat after every segment or main idea. This movement provides a visual transition. Again, it allows your body to support the transitions associated with your speech. Movement is an excellent way to connect with members of the audience. It is very necessary in extemp speaking. However, do not pace. That is distracting. It diverts attention from your speech. The judge becomes hypnotized by your body movement. Also, do not walk right up to the judge's desk in your quest for movement. Judges often find that approach uncomfortable and intimidating. Extempers should also not appear stiff and rigid when moving. A natural and spontaneous manner of movement will make you and your audience comfortable with your delivery.

Your goal is to be **fluent**. If you are having problems with "uhs" and other distracting speech patterns, practice more before tournaments. With hard work, you can overcome fluency problems. Once you achieved fluency, you will always have it in extemp. Again be patient with yourself. Few are fluent when they begin extemp. After all, you are analyzing public policy. You have never discussed such complex issues before. With practice, you can do it!

Establish **eye contact** with your audience, especially the judge or judges. If there are three judges, look at all three judges, not the one you prefer to look at. All three will rank you. Do not look at the wall over the tops of the heads of the judges. It also looks foolish. Direct eye contact is the key to sustaining the judge's attention. Remember, you are trying to sustain their attention, while trying to earn their acceptance. You must establish eye contact with the audience.

Delivery will improve with practice. It will not be mastered overnight. But my, how you will dazzle the judges once you get a handle on the fundamentals of extemp. You will amaze yourself and your audiences.

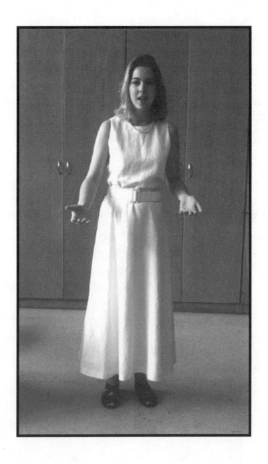

TOP NINE TIPS FOR SUCCESS IN EXTEMPORANEOUS SPEAKING

1. Begin an extemp file. Read, cut, and copy articles from newspapers and magazines on current events.

2. Watch news programs that provide analysis of current events.

3. Answer extemp questions based upon the precise wording of the question.

4. Pick extemp questions that you are familiar with and that your judge will find worthwhile.

5. Learn the elements of organization. The introduction should gain attention, announce the question, and preview main ideas. The body should develop the main ideas with analysis and evidence from your file. The conclusion should review main ideas explaining clearly how you have answered the question and then provide a clincher often connecting to the attention getter.

6. Use the thirty minute prep time wisely, choosing the question, quickly reading pertinent files, writing the outline to your speech, and practicing the speech before the actual presentation.

7. Practice, practice, practice! Try to give practice speeches several times a week. The key to fluency is continual practice.

8. Try to develop an appropriate pace for the delivery. Develop natural gestures used on important points. Practice body movement at points of transition. Establish eye contact with your audience.

9. A reminder: be patient with yourself as you learn the art of extemp.

ACTIVITIES

1. Meet with other extempers on your squad. Make a group list of current news events. Share your thoughts and perception of those stories. Ask questions of those who seem to be familiar with certain events. Novices should learn much from experienced extempers.

2. Make a list of important news stories both domestically and internationally. Divide up the labor among yourself in researching those areas. Find out if anyone has subscriptions to magazines. Find out which ones your coach takes. Discover which sources can be found in the school library. Try to work as a team to make a comprehensive file.

3. If you are a novice, have your coach or experienced extemper write a question for you. Take twenty-four hours to study it. Write a speech answering the question. In the beginning, take your time learning about the extemp areas. Don't rush to meet the thirty minute time frame until you are familiar with the areas and understand the elements of an extemp speech.

4. Meet at an extempers home and watch a newscast. Afterwards, discuss the big stories. Share your opinions with each other. Try to debate the issues presented in the newscast. Note also communication qualities about the broadcasters. Did they use gestures? If so, what type? What was their rate of speech? Look also at a television guide. Make a list of news programs for the oncoming week. Divide up the job of watching the news shows. Meet again in a week to compare notes. Make a list of the better programs to watch on a continual basis.

CHAPTER 4

Expository

After completing this chapter you should be able to:

❏ Define expository speaking

❏ Select an expository topic

❏ Organize an expository speech

❏ Utilize outlining as a guide to organization

❏ Use effective techniques of delivery

❏ Memorize a speech and realize the value of rehearsal

New Terms To Learn In This Chapter

Brainstorming

Speech Structure

Informative

Outlining

THE NATURE OF EXPOSITORY SPEAKING

Perhaps the most common type of speaking used by humans is expository, or speaking that explains. By our very nature we want to share our knowledge and experiences with others. When we read an interesting article in the paper or in a magazine, we often relate the important details to our friends and family. Most of us are not content with just knowing things. We instinctively feel compelled to pass on what we have learned to others. However, we are very selective about what we share. We rarely get pleasure in telling someone something he already knows. We also rarely communicate ideas that someone else might not find interesting. For most of us, we communicate ideas that are truly **informative**.

By definition an expository speech is one in which the speaker provides a learning experience for the listener by presenting new information in an interesting manner. If the listener does not learn something new, then the speaker has not informed the listener. That is not to say that you can not speak on a common topic. For as long as new information is being shared, then the speech meets the criteria for expository. The speech should also be written in an interesting manner. The quality of the research and the writing ability play key roles in measuring how interesting the speech may be to the listener.

Although there is not an exact formula to determine what interests human beings, there are some important indicators. Obviously, we all have diverse interests. What one person finds fascinating, the next person finds boring. The competitive speaker must search for elements of universality in the choice of topic. Consider the popular news programs on television. Such shows are successful because they pick subjects that viewers find interesting. If the programs focus on topics that are boring or repetitive, few would watch them. The producers of such programs tend to enlighten us with either a new look at an old topic or an insightful view of a new topic. If the programs fail to inform the public, the programs can be canceled by the network. Similarly, the expository speaker who fails to inform his audience will fail to meet the central objective of this type of speaking.

Because human beings are not simply processors of information, we must be entertained to some extent. New information alone may not captivate our attention. You must look for ways to add some spice to your speech. Humor is often an effective way to keep the attention of the audience. A cleverly written pun or anecdote in the introduction may help the judge remember your speech. On the other hand, an overuse of humor may detract from the main points you are trying to communicate. Humor can be used to sustain attention and to reinforce the main ideas presented in the speech.

An expository speech will be successful when the speech critic exclaims on the ballot, "That was fascinating!" If the listener learned something new and learned it in an interesting manner, the listener will have a more favorable reaction to the speech. The key to success in this event is found in the inherent definition of expository. If you present worthwhile information in an interesting manner, you will be on the track of success in this event.

HOW TO SELECT A TOPIC

Getting started is often the most frustrating part of the speech process. Many students ask their coach, "Can you suggest a winning topic?" The coach often points to the library. Coaches want you to find your own topic. Our jobs are far more interesting when we are informed on fresh topics. What a state champion discussed five years ago, may not work for you. Topics can often become dated. There are many ways to select a topic.

CONSULT YOUR OWN INTERESTS

What interests you? Your personal interests may spark the enthusiasm for a sensational speech. Your enthusiasm for a topic is key in the necessary motivation to write the speech. If you write on a topic suggested by someone else, you may be headed down a long, desolate road never reaching the destination. Within all of us is a myriad of thoughts and experiences that may stimulate the idea for a fantastic expository speech. But given the complexity of the human mind, how can we extract the best ideas? One proven method is:

BRAINSTORMING

Do not overlook the value of brainstorming. It is simply a way to explore your mind to see if a topic can be randomly found. It may not sound scientific. But it has worked for many speakers. With expository, ask yourself one question, "What topics do I know about that could be informative to an audience?" Think of every possible idea to answer that question. Do not rule anything out. Write every thought on a sheet of paper.

The following example demonstrates this process. First, make a list of two types of subjects.

SERIOUS!   NOT SO SERIOUS!

At the beginning of the process, you may not be sure you want to find the meaning of the universe or just dazzle the audience with wit and creativity. OK, let's get:

SERIOUS	NOT SO SERIOUS
Computers/ Internet	The Origin Of Popcorn
Advances In Medicine	Astrology (What's Your Sign?)
Health/ Fitness	Fad Diets (It's Worth A Try)
History	The VW Beetle (Why Was It So
Famous People	Popular? What A Weird
Dreams	Looking Car! I Sure Loved
Sleep Deprivation	Mine.)
Right Brain/Left Brain (Which Side	Breakfast Cereals
Am I Using Now? Oh It Doesn't	TV Talk Shows, Who Cares?
Matter Or Does It? Let's Go On!)	Hot Peppers
Environment	Spam Light (A Contradiction In
Recycling (Should I Recycle This	Terms)
Sheet Of Paper Or Keep	The Yo Yo
Thinking?)	Hula Hoops
Stress (I Feel It Right Now! I Must	Imagination (I Could Use It Now!
Find A Topic!)	I Seem To Be Drifting Back To
	Reality)

Go ahead! Make your own list through the process of brainstorming. See how many topics you can think of in five minutes. Once your list is made, you must realize that there is distinctive difference between a **subject** and a **topic**. A subject is very broad and would not be suitable for a five to seven minute speech. Consider the subject of computers. There are many aspects of computers. You would have to narrow the focus to a specific aspect of computers, in order to adequately develop the topic. You might discuss how computers are changing education or how they are changing our daily lives.

Brainstorming is much like word association. You may think of one word and then think of other words that are associated with the original word.

For example I play the guitar. If I write a speech about the guitar, I might use brainstorming or word association to narrow my focus to guitar terms such as electric, lace sensor pickups, Fender, Gibson, single-double cut-away, tuning keys, guitar amplifiers, vintage guitars, or the guitar's role in the popularity of rock and country music. From just one thought, I came up with many possible topics that could be used from the general subject of guitars.

Although brainstorming may help you to envision a topic, the quality of research will have a greater impact on topic selection. An expository speech can not be very informative without:

RESEARCH

Before making a decision on your topic, research your two or three preferred topics. The key to a good speech is pertinent information. Research as many periodicals or books as you can after selecting a topic. The more perspectives you discover, the more selective choices you can make in the inclusion of interesting data for your speech. Novice speech writers often base most of their speech on one article. This makes the speech little more than a grade school "report." An effective speech is a careful blending of facts and perspectives coupled with your own insight into the nature of a phenomenon.

A student once wrote a speech on "hiccups". He found one article that focused on a man that had the hiccups for his entire life. Although he claimed that he could not find any other sources on the topic, he felt that the man's story could still captivate the audience's attention. The judges were amused but not informed in comparison to the more substantially researched speeches. Another student speaking on "hiccups" focused on the various remedies to stop the hiccups such as placing a bag over one's head. The humor created by the description of such methods and the visual enactment of these methods entertained and informed the audience. Selection of a good speech topic is not the only consideration that matters in the speech process. It is the information provided that makes the difference between an average speech and the speech that captivates the audience.

Books may also be helpful, but may overload the writer with too much information. The expository speech is a relatively short speech. Too much information can cause you to feel overwhelmed and frustrated in the speech process. Remember also that a speech is not a term paper. It is a combination of your original thoughts based upon selected research. A novice student wrote his first expository speeches on left handed people. This was a topic that he knew well because he was a "lefty." He had a wealth of information stored in his memory, based on his childhood experiences. He recalled the challenge of writing in elementary school desks designed for right-handed students. He was called "wrong handed" by classmates and was generally discriminated against, until his baseball coach pointed out the advantage of left-handed hitting on his little league team. He also did historical research and discussed several famous people that were left-handed, such as Napoleon and John F. Kennedy. His speech balanced personal experience, a sense of humor, and pertinent research.

BROWSING

A more intuitive approach to topic selection is simply to browse through your library or favorite book store. You just might find a book title or magazine title that will give you the idea for a fantastic expository. Keep an open mind and consider all the possibilities. Many students can get a quick start through browsing, especially in expository speaking. The informative implication of this speech allows for almost any topic explained in magazines or books. It is basically a more intuitive method but may work for you.

A WORD OF CAUTION ON TOPIC SELECTION

Avoid picking topics from television news shows. Your speech judge may have watched the same show. It would be redundant for the judge, not informative. Avoid topics that the print media are emphasizing. Select topics that are not everyday stories. You will seldom risk repetition if your topic is not a conversation piece at the typical American dinner table. Use your imagination and research skills to come up with a speech topic that will benefit you and your audience.

WRITING YOUR EXPOSITORY

ORGANIZATION

After completing your research, the next stage in the process is the writing of an outline. If you write the speech without outlining first, you will spend more time revising and actually spend more time on the composition stage. **Outlining** will enable you to develop the main points of your speech. Outlining is critical in the organization of the speech. Even the most skilled speaker will not succeed without organization of thought.

There are three components of a **speech's structure** that demand careful attention in your preliminary outline:

THE INTRODUCTION, THE BODY, THE CONCLUSION

A clear conception of each of the three parts will enable you to compose a well organized speech that your audience will follow and understand.

THE INTRODUCTION

The introduction is a critical part of your speech. If you do not get the attention and interest in the topic from the beginning, it is difficult to sustain interest in the remainder of the speech. Never start off by directly stating your topic. If you begin by saying, "My speech is on dreams," your audience may respond by thinking, "Not another speech on dreams!" Therefore, you must think of the best method of gaining attention. With the topic of "dreams," you might begin by describing a dream that you can recall. As you describe this dream, your audience will be listening with keen interest, wondering where this experience is headed. After a relativity brief description (20 or 30 seconds,) inform the judge that the experience you were describing was only a dream, not a part of reality. Now you have the attention of your judge. He is ready to be informed on the nature of dreaming.

> Forms Of Attention Getters:
>
> ➤ Analogy
> ➤ Startling or shocking statement

➤ Direct quotation
➤ Humorous anecdote
➤ Illustration
➤ Hypothetical story or example
➤ Real life story or example
➤ Reference to the subject or occasion

The choice of opening depends on the nature of your speech. A lighter topic, somewhat humorous speech, requires a humorous anecdote. A more serious topic such as a "cure for a disease," might require a dramatic story of a person suffering from the disease. A speech on politicians might benefit from a clever analogy. The real key to the opening is **creativity**. Use you imagination to select the opening that fits the topic. One student wrote a speech on "stuttering." He began his speech by stuttering his way through the opening. After a few sentences delivered with much difficulty, the judges often showed signs of sympathy with a nonverbal response signifying encouragement. They were thinking, "Come on young man. You can do it!" At that point, he switched gears and exclaimed in a very well-modulated voice, "Although I was just pretending, many people must learn to understand and overcome problems associated with stuttering." His opening grabbed the attention of the judge and allowed the speaker to present the medical facts about stuttering. Without the opening, the speech might have been too dry for the audience. To be sure, the suspense opener can be an effective method of drawing the audience into the speech.

After presenting the attention getter, it can be useful to answer the question: "**Why listen** to the speech?" One might discuss how the subject affects the audience in terms of their health, security, happiness, or any other interest or need. Refer to Chapter Two's description of the motivated sequence for other ideas. [Chapter 2, p. 22]

Next, make a clear **thesis statement**. It should be a concise description of the topic. Describe exactly what you will be discussing. An organized speaker will formulate a clearly worded statement of topic for the purpose of clarity.

Next, **preview the main points** of the speech. This should be limited to three points. The number of points may vary depending on the type of topic. By providing the audience with a brief picture of where you are heading, they are better able to follow your progression of ideas.

THE BODY

The main points of the speech should be organized as they were previewed in the introduction. When establishing the key areas, it is important to consider some different methods of organization.

Chronological order is an effective method of organization in many expository speeches. If your topic describes a process or depicts an event in history, a time order works very well. A speech on the origin of the game "monopoly" would begin with the origin of the inventor's initial idea, proceed to the marketing stage, and conclude with the overwhelming success of the game.

Cause and effect is another popular form of organization. This pattern of organization explains how one thing or event prompts another to occur. A speech on understanding the causes of homelessness might identify poverty, lack of government programs, and mental illness as some major causes of homelessness.

Topic order is useful for speeches that divide the topic into subcategories. A speaker can move from most important to least important, or from least important to most important. A speech on how physical fitness can improve health might discuss benefits such as improved cardiovascular fitness, improved sleep, and weight control.

Whatever method of organization that you choose, try to use a variety of *support materials* on each point. Support materials may include illustrations, specific examples, or statistics.

THE CONCLUSION

Now that you have completed your planning of the introduction and body, it is time to plan another important part of the speech, the conclusion. The conclusion is key in insuring that the audience remembers your speech after the round. In this segment you should first **review the main points**. You may also draw any conclusions you wish to make about your topic. The conclusion should end with a clincher statement that provides closure to the speech. A common method is tying the speech together by connecting the ending to the opening. The speaker discussing the "dream" topic could go back to his opening dream and describe it further. The speaker would then take the audience back to the dream world described in the introduction. Others may choose a direct quote from an authority or famous person.

The competitive expository speaker must have a creative introduction, a well structured body, and a fitting conclusion. When the three parts are prepared well, success in expository can be achieved.

Let us review what we have learned about the organizational structure by viewing them in an outline format.

I. Introduction

    A. Attention step
    B. Thesis statement
    C. Relevance of topic to audience
    D. Preview of main points
       1. First main point
       2. Second main point
       3. Third main point

II. Body

    A. First main point
       1. supporting detail
       2.   "
    B. Second main point
       1. supporting detail
       2.   "
    C. Third main point
       1. supporting detail
       2.   "

III. Conclusion

    A. Review topic
    B. Review main points and draw conclusions
    C. Clincher

A speech outline should be as detailed as possible. After all, you are developing the general framework of your speech text. You should use complete sentences for the most part. All supporting detail should further develop main points. Show your outline to your coach before writing the text of the speech. He may spot some organizational problems that you can correct before you write the rough draft of the speech.

Many speech writers write the body of the outline first. The main points must be written before you can preview them in the introduction. You can plan the opening more specifically, if you know the direction you are going to take in the body of the speech.

The following outline was written for an expository speech. Read the outline and check how closely the writer meets the speech structure previously explained.

SAMPLE EXPOSITORY OUTLINE

I. Introduction

    A. "My obsession with the safety of my daughter grew so great that every time I started to seal an envelope, I had to repeatedly check to make sure I hadn't trapped her inside."

    B. These pitiful words come from a man suffering from Obsessive Compulsive Disorder, or OCD.

    C. Because there is a bit of compulsion in all of us, it is important that we understand the difference between normal obsession and abnormal obsession.

    D. In examining this condition I will discuss three areas:
        1. the definition of OCD
        2. treatment of OCD

II. Body

    A. What is OCD?
        1. clinical definition
        2. compulsive types of OCD
            a. compulsive hand washing
            b. ritualistic eating habits

    B. What is a treatment for OCD?
        1. Psychological treatment
            a. systematic desensitization
            b. encounter groups
        2. physiological treatment
            a. Valium
            b. Lithium

III. Conclusion

    A. As you can see, OCD is a serious and complex condition.

    B. Today, I have answered three questions about OCD.

    C. So the next time you start to seal an envelope, remember that if you stop to make sure that no one is inside, you too may suffer from Obsessive Compulsive Disorder.

WRITING THE SPEECH

Writing the speech is the most critical segment of the speech process. Without a quality speech even the greatest of speakers is headed for failure. Solid writing skills are truly necessary in competitive speech. An effective writer uses language that is original and meaningful. Creativity, imagination, and wit are also important in the writing of a speech. When a student turns in a well-written rough draft to me, I know that he or she is going to have a positive experience in expository. When a student turns in a weak rough draft, full of grammatical errors and unclear sentences, I know that it may take a considerable amount of work before that student's work is acceptable for presentation. Speech writers should always take composition seriously. Your English classes and other subjects that require accurate writing should be of the utmost importance to you.

Your coach will give you a time line for writing the rough draft of your speech. It is important that you make some revisions of your own before handing it in to the coach. Your coach will then critique the manuscript, making constructive comments for you to consider for your final draft. Your coach may suggest that grammatical corrections need to be made or that something is still lacking in the speech. Do not feel discouraged if the negative comments seem to outweigh the positive. Remember that your coach has your success in mind. Make the necessary corrections quickly. If you disagree with some of the comments, share your feelings with your coach. He or she may see it your way or further explain the basis for the criticism. You should realize too, that your coach has had far more experience with the nature of individual events competition. After the revisions are made to the satisfaction of your coach, you are ready for the next phase of the process: the delivery.

TECHNIQUES OF DELIVERY

THE PRESENTATION

The tone of expository speaking should be one that lends itself to an objective presentation. Your delivery should not sound persuasive as in original oratory. It should sound like you are teaching your audience an interesting lesson. News reporters try to deliver the news in an objective manner. They try to communicate the information and allow the audience to formulate a reaction to the news events. Similarly, the delivery of the expository speech should be nonemotional, yet presented with a contagious level of interest in the topic. In other words the judge should perceive your interest in this topic by the way you deliver the speech.

Variation is also important in expository. You should not sound like a computerized message on an answering machine. You will bore your audience to tears. Variety is the key in effective vocal techniques. Variate the pace. It is a mistake to use the same rhythm throughout the speech. An effective speaker will slow down on phrases and pick up the pace on others. Pauses need to be used for effect as well. Timing is critical in speech delivery. Variate the pitch of your voice. A monotone delivery, for a speech of any length, will not be acceptable to the audience. The volume also needs variety. Be a little loud or soft, never the same throughout the speech. The attention of the audience is kept through a variety of vocal techniques.

The physical aspects of delivery are critical to success. You should appear relaxed during your presentation. Hands should be at the sides of the body. Gestures are used to make important points. Beginning speakers often fail to use gestures, making them appear rigid and nervous. Speakers should not let their voices do all of the communicating. Effective gestures need to extend away from the body towards the audience. Gestures often reveal the palms of your hands. Gestures should also appear natural, as in the gesturing that we use in conversations with friends. Never overuse gestures. They can be distracting and will actually defeat the purpose of using gestures in the first place. A gesture enhances and reinforces what you are verbally communicating.

Movement is also important. The expository speaker should not stand in one place for the duration of the speech. After the introduction, take a step or two to the right or left. Move again as you make a transition to a new point. It is a visual transition for the audience. Movement is a way to support speech transitions. It also allows you to more effectively connect with members of the audience. Movement must also be natural. You should not appear stiff and rigid in the attempt to move in your speeches. Movement should make you and the audience feel more comfortable.

Eye contact is critical in the communication process. Without eye contact, you can not keep the attention of the audience. Remember, you are communicating to them, not at them. You should always look at the members of the audience during a speech, as in any type of interpersonal communication.

Effective speakers also possess enthusiasm. You should demonstrate a desire to present your speech. Enthusiasm is very contagious. If you are enthusiastic about your presentation, then your judge will be enthusiastic about listening to you. Enthusiasm can be noticeable in your voice as well as in your eyes. It can be shown by the way you walk to the front of the room when you begin and the way in which you leave the room. Make every speech presentation important. Remember that this may be the first and only time your judge will hear your speech. If you act like you have given this speech too many times, the lack of enthusiasm will be evident. You are offering a message to the world in individual events competition. It is truly exciting and you should take advantage of this wonderful opportunity in your life.

MEMORIZATION AND REHEARSAL

Many students feel that they can not memorize a three or four page manuscript. If you are one of those, I assure you that you can memorize your speech. The real fear comes from the fact that we are seldom challenged to memorize anything of length. With effort, you can memorize your speech. With repeated practice in class or at tournaments, you will not forget your speech.

Here are some tips for learning your speech. Carry the script with you at all times. Read it over and over. Think about the progression of the paragraphs. The order of the speech should be logical to you. You are the author. Go paragraph by paragraph until you have it completely memorized. Practice in a variety of settings. Give your speech in the car, the shower, or in the back yard. Present it to your brothers, sisters, or parents. You can not practice enough. At tournaments do not be shy. Talk to the lockers or practice in unused rooms. Memorization is probably the most simplistic part of the entire speech process. You can do it with a little effort and patience. And once you learn it, you will dazzle the audience with the way you can present, word for word, your expository speech.

Remember to continue the rehearsal after you have competed. If you assume you will always remember the speech, you may be surprised when you perform at the next tournament. The human memory bank often requires recharging. The rehearsal process will slow down after the speech is learned; but it must continue throughout the season for continued success.

TOP NINE TIPS FOR SUCCESS IN EXPOSITORY

1. Develop a solid understanding of the possibilities of expository.

2. After much brainstorming and careful thought, select a topic that you like and one your audience will benefit from and also enjoy.

3. After researching your topic, write a complete outline of your speech.

4. Focus on developing a creative introduction and a fitting conclusion.

5. Write a rough draft following the progress of ideas detailed in the outline.

6. Pay careful attention to the selection of words and phrases in your speech.

7. Submit a typed copy to your coach for critical comments. After making revisions that meet your coach's approval, memorize the text of the speech.

8. Study the elements of effective delivery.

9. Practice your speech until you know it well!

ACTIVITIES

1. Break up into small groups and brainstorm for topics. Try establishing categories for the topics such as science, personal, fads, history, humorous, serious, or shocking. Each person in the group may think of a category. Take ten minutes to think of at least twenty topics for each category. Each group should share their list with the class.

2. The following is a list of topics generated by brainstorming. Pick the ones you like and research them. Discuss with members of your class which topics would work and which ones would not make good expository topics. What characteristics are common in a weak topic? What characteristics make a topic strong?

Tipping, Cartoons, Winnie the Pooh, Origami, Barbie Dolls, Tarot Cards, Mythology, Astrology, Couch Potatoism, Weird College Scholarships, Rainbows, Jewelry, Bugs, Boxers, Chocolate, Computers, Cats, Dogs, Clouds, America's Obsession with Health Food, Junk Food, Vampires, Sibling Rivalry, Imagination.

Refer to your own list of topics from exercise one. Apply the same questions to your own list. Then, revise your list of topics deleting the weak topics. Carefully examine the better topics for consideration in the selection process.

3. Delivery exercises will enhance your concentration. I once had a student present his speech while lying on the floor. Try giving your speech in unusual positions and locations. Practice in noisy settings like the school cafeteria. Have your friends distract you with facial expressions.

There are many distractions at tournaments. Competitors may peer through the window of the door to see if you are done. An actor may be performing a loud dramatic interpretation in the adjoining room. Concentration is critical to success in individual events competition. As a student once said in his speech, "Concentration is the excuse for the win-less, and the reason for champions."

Impromptu Speaking

After completing this chapter you should be able to:

❏ Define impromptu speaking

❏ Understand and use organizational strategies for an impromptu speech

❏ Present an impromptu speech on a proverb, quotation, or word

❏ Speak with ease on many topics with limited preparation

New Terms To Learn In This Chapter

Limited Preparation

Proverbs

Kernel

Abstract Words

IMPROMPTU SPEAKING

Impromptu speaking is one of the most challenging and interesting speech events. It is similar to extemporaneous in that one draws a topic and speaks on the topic for the round. However, impromptu is a very limited preparation event. One has to learn to speak, only minutes after drawing the topic. Forensics competitors find this event to be a true test of the "gift of gab," and a great deal of fun as well!

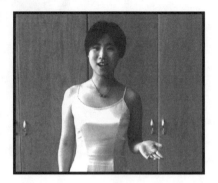

The National Forensic League offers the following explanation on the impromptu speaking ballot. It states:

> The Impromptu speech should be regarded as an original interpretation by the speaker of the designated topic as supported by varied materials and gives a contestant opportunity to be creative and imaginative. An impromptu speech should reveal the student's ability to organize his thoughts quickly and in a logical manner.

> The contestant should be held accountable for strict adherence to the topic drawn and discounted severely for shifting to some other topic on which s/he might prefer to speak. The information presented should be well-chosen, pertinent, and sufficient to support the central thought of the topic.

> The material should be organized according to some logical plan to produce a complete speech within the time allowed. Delivery should be free from marked defects in the mechanics of speech-poise, quality and use of voice, enunciation, fluency, bodily expressiveness-and should be effective in enlisting and holding the interest of the audience.

> The best impromptu speech combines clear thinking, good speaking, and interesting presentation with respect to the subject chosen. Notes are not permitted.

> There is no minimum qualifying time. Do not penalize a contestant for brevity unless he fails to cover his subject adequately. Maximum time is five minutes. Impose no penalty for overtime unless it is excessive.

> There will be a five-minute preparation time. Impromptu topics will be chosen from proverbs, ordinary things, abstract words, events, quotations, and famous people.

That description provides an excellent starting ground for the impromptu speaker. Essentially impromptu is a **limited preparation** event. It is similar to extemporaneous in that one draws a topic and must speak on that topic shortly. Impromptu is not, however, necessarily the study of current events. The preparation time is very short compared to the thirty minutes in extemporaneous speaking. A student should get a good understanding of what to do in the speech before attempting this event. Some impromptu speakers sound like extempers making references to books and magazines. Some are totally personal, discussing anecdotes from their lives. Many combine elements of both academic content and personal references.

The *format* of impromptu varies from state to state. A common form consists of a five minute prep time and a five minute speaking time. Another popular format is a seven minute prep and speaking time combined. For example one might use one and one-half minutes to prepare and five and one-half minutes to speak. Other states provide one minute to select the topic, one minute to prepare, and five to speak.

The *topic* can be proverbs, quotations, words, objects, people, or other forms of language that can be interpreted. Whatever the topic is, one should use his own knowledge in constructing a speech analyzing the topic.

Strategies for writing the speech include the following elements. Address the topic via showing significance to the audience. You can do this by personalizing the topic through your analysis. Demonstrate how your topic may affect each of our lives or the role it may play. Using the idea of "personal significance" as a main idea, general structure might be developed in the following way.

I. Introduction

    A. Attention getter
    B. Preview of major points

II. Body

    A. First area of analysis
       1. example
       2. explanation/relevance to topic
    (Repeat for sub-point B and C)

III. Conclusion

    A. Review of major points
    B. Refer back to attention getter and conclude

Now let us look what can be included in each component of the impromptu speech. Consider first the body and areas of analysis. There are a number of directions one can go in selecting areas of analysis. One possible structure is to focus on the possible **benefits/harms** of the topic. This can be very effective for topics based on concepts (i.e. freedom, motivation, justice, poverty). You can provide the point of view as your major topic area and then give an example to back up or prove your point. Consider the following example on the topic of "freedom."

I. Intro

    A. Attention getter-provide an example showing how freedom may have an impact on our lives. Also, briefly introduce the topic and state your view of its overall significance.

    B. Preview-list, in order, the headings of your major points. In this case, your points might be how freedom can be beneficial on an individual basis, and how it may be harmful, and how it may be beneficial to society as a whole.

II. Body

    A. How freedom may benefit the individual
        1. give a basic overview of the concept
        2. provide an example to back up your analysis
        3. restate your basic thesis and explain relevance of example to topic

    B. How freedom may be harmful at times
        (repeat steps 1-3 above for first point)

    C. How freedom is generally beneficial to society
        (repeat steps 1-3 above)

III. Conclusion

    A. Restate topic and reiterate that it is significant to all of us
    B. Review major points
    C. Refer back to attention-getter in concluding statement.

Another way to organize is to label your areas of analysis as the *example* which you are going to talk about. This method may not give the impression of an in-depth method of analysis as compared to the first method.

With this approach you do not have to take a stance on the topic. However, it is important to give the judge/audience a reason to listen, and creating the significance underlying the topic may do this.

There are many forms of *examples*. Examples may come in the form of anecdotes, stories, or trivia. Many prefer to utilize examples which come from their own experience and knowledge. **Personal experiences** are the most obvious place to get examples. It is probably best to use just one per speech. One strategy is to use personal experiences in the introduction, followed by more standard examples for the other points.

There are innumerable additional categories for examples. **Philosophy** has been popular on the collegiate level. It enables a speaker to establish a value criteria for analyzing a topic. The **Historical** example is also quite popular. History is full of examples for a view on any topic. It is important, however, to have your facts straight. Inaccurate descriptions of historical data will not please your audience. **Literary** examples are another popular type of example. Literature is full of examples to exemplify topics. Consider plays, novels, short stories, or poems. Other areas may include politics, current events, sports, or movies. When using examples, remember to relate examples to the topic and/or the stance you are establishing in your speech. Also, make sure that you make them interesting. Analysis is important but you need to grab and hold the interest of the audience through examples.

HOW TO DEAL WITH PROVERBS OR QUOTATIONS

In addition to abstract concepts, many tournaments offer famous proverbs and quotations. This presents a more difficult challenge. It is much easier to deal with one word or concept rather than an entire sentence. Hence, it is a good idea to base the speech on your interpretation of the quotation, rather than attempting to deal with the entire quotation itself. Such an interpretation should be extremely brief (one word, a short phrase) and should be very clearly worded. Interpretation should really focus on the central meaning or "heart" of the quotation. It can be called the "**kernel**," as in the central, essential part.

The kernel should be established and reaffirmed throughout your speech. Link your examples and analysis to your kernel. Simultaneously, you should link your kernel back to the quotation. This will help with clarity and also further convince the judge that your interpretation of the quotation is correct. Although there may be several possible kernels within a quotation, find the one that best represents your interpretation of the quotation. Any interpretation of a quotation is legitimate as long as it is a reasonable development of the quotation and is justified within your speech. The kernel should be no more than one or two words, or a brief phrase. Such a limitation helps with the clarity of your speech and it also gives a very specific focus. It is advisable to choose a kernel that shows some sort of holistic analysis of the quotation. Do not pick any word. Be selective in the interpretation.

Sample quotation:

> "I may disapprove of what you say, but I will defend to the death your right to say it." — Voltaire.

Possible kernels on Voltaire's quote might be:

- Freedom of speech
- Freedom
- Open mindedness
- Respecting others
- Common enemies

After you have determined what the central theme (kernel) is, structure your speech as you would normally around that topic.[1]

Unified analysis also applies to impromptu speaking.[2] All information presented by the speaker should provide justification or support of the thesis. A vital step in impromptu is extrapolating a thesis. With a quotation, phrase, or proverb, one must provide an interpretation. If the topic is a word, one must define and explain it. If the topic is a person or place, the speaker must briefly identify who, where or what it is and explain why it is important.

Here Is A Second Example Of Structure For The Impromptu Speech

I. Introduction
   A. Attention–Getter

---

[1] Brian White, Coach at Buhler High School and former member of the Wichita State University I.E. Squad.
[2] Robert Carroll, "An Introduction to Impromptu Speaking," to be published in *Rostrum*.

B. Lead in to Topic
C. Statement of Topic
D. Thesis (interpret/define/identify the topic)
E. Preview (for two reasons: A and B)

II. Reason A
A. Explanation of Logic
B. Example to Illustrate
C. Another example to illustrate
D. Discussion of the relationship of the examples to each other and to the topic

III. Reason B
A. Explanation of Logic
B. Example to Illustrate
C. Another example to Illustrate
D. Discussion of the relationship of the examples to each other and to the topic

IV. Conclusion
A. Review Statement
B. Restatement of Topic
C. Restatement of Thesis
D. Restatement of Attention Getter

Here Are Examples Of Structures For Impromptu Speeches

Type of topic: famous person

Name: Jerry Garcia
Thesis: Jerry Garcia, the recently deceased vocalist/songwriter/ guitarist for the band **The Grateful Dead**, was a significant figure in contemporary American society:
    I. Because he was an influential musician.
    II. Because he lived a self-destructive lifestyle.

Type of topic: place

Place: Mount Everest
Thesis: Mount Everest, the highest mountain in the world, is a significant place in the world:

    I. Because it is isolated from most of humankind.

    II. Because it is extremely dangerous to climb.

Type of topic: word

Word: Liberty

Thesis: Liberty is the freedom from control and the right to act on your own:

    I. Because it signifies freedom for individuals, it implies people are not subject to absolute restrictions from the state.

    II. Because it signifies responsibility for one's own actions, it implies people may act in their own best interest.

Type of topic: proverb

Proverb: Revenge is a dish best served cold.

Thesis: Revenge is best achieved in a cold-blooded manner:

    I. Because revenge is not taken in the heat of the moment — it is planned.

    II. Because revenge is not a crime of passion — it is a crime of retribution.[3]

Impromptu speaking will enhance your creative potential through its emphasis on spontaneity. Like extemp, it helps you to improve your fluency by speaking without previous preparation. Practice with proverb or quotation books, or make a list of **abstract words** such as freedom, hate, or envy. Study a bit of history; keep up on current events; read literature carefully in your English classes; and just be informed about the world around you, from the lives and careers of movie stars, to the political figures that run our world.

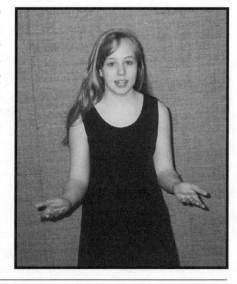

[3] Robert Carroll

REVIEW

TOP NINE TIPS FOR SUCCESS IN IMPROMPTU SPEAKING

1. Begin reading books of quotations or proverbs.

2. Make a list of abstract words to interpret.

3. When writing an impromptu speech, show how your topic affects the lives of your audience.

4. Study the three part structure of an impromptu speech. It should have an introduction, body, and conclusion.

5. Realize that the main areas of analysis can be either showing the benefits/harms of the topic or by showing examples of the topic.

6. Examples can be found in personal experiences, philosophy, history, literature, or in current events.

7. Proverbs need to be interpreted in one word or short phrase.

8. Practice determining the "kernel" of the quotation.

9. Practice giving impromptu speeches with peers or your coach.

ACTIVITIES

1. Make a list of words and quotations. As a class, try writing sample speech outlines on the same topics. Share your outline with the class. This will demonstrate the many creative ways a topic can be approached in impromptu.

2. Ask one of your peers to write a topic for you. Give a speech to your peer. Then reverse the process and write one for your peer. He or she should then deliver a speech to you.

SAMPLE TOPICS and WORDS

Remembering your childhood.	The random	The abstract
	Cannibalism	
Monopoly	Paper	Sanitized
Dr. Seuss	Cults	Light
Scrambled Eggs	Mouse traps	Finances
Checkers	Tabloids	Hibernation
Father	Fossil	Violation
Band Aids	Bootleg	Listen
Wallpaper	DNA	Gambling
Candy	Blindfolded	Understanding
Frisbee	Army	Thought
Haircut	Signature	Freedom
Questions	Tranquilized	Responsibility
Respect	Wheelchair	Infinity
Plaid	Deja vu	Virtue
Cotton	Imagination	Marriage
Denim	Altruism	Routine
Music	Apathy	

QUOTATIONS

"There are two tragedies in life. One is not to get your heart's desire. The other is to get it." — George Bernard Shaw

All things are less dreadful than they seem.

Zeal is fit only for wise men but is found mostly in fools.

A book that is shut is but a block.

Don't hang a man and then try him afterward.

A cloud can not cast a shadow unless the sun is shining.

"I disapprove of what you say, but I will defend to death your right to say it." — Voltaire

"I have great faith in fools- my friends call it self-confidence." — Edgar Allen Poe

"Most of the time I don't have much fun, the rest of the time I don't have any fun at all." — Woody Allen

"Always forgive your enemies; nothing annoys them so much." — Oscar Wilde

"Man is a political animal." — Aristotle

"You can be on the right track, but if you sit there too long, you'll get run over." — Will Rogers

"There's a big difference between good, sound reasoning, and reasoning that sounds good." — Burton Hillis

"A man always has two reasons for doing anything — a good reason, and the real reason." — J.P. Morgan

PART TWO

DRAMATIC INTERPRETATION
HUMOROUS INTERPRETATION
PROSE AND POETRY
INTERPRETATION
DUET ACTING
IMPROVISED DUET ACTING
DUO INTERPRETATION

DRAMA EVENTS

CHAPTER

6

Dramatic Interpretation

● ●
●
●

After completing this chapter you should be able to:

❏ Identify selection elements for dramatic interpretation

❏ Recognize the effects of stance on characterization

❏ Memorize using a variety of methods

❏ Prepare introductions that are informative and creative

❏ Develop strong characterizations through script analysis

New Terms To Learn In This Chapter

Monotone	Text Analysis
Stance	Sub-Text Analysis
Inflection	Personal Business
Pace	Voice
Character Blending	Pitch

DRAMATIC INTERPRETATION

Jokingly, it is sometimes said that you must have qualities of a split personality to play an interpretative event, or that you must be a deeply depressed or a masochistic person to choose such melancholy situations to repeat over and over in dramatic interpretation competition. Of course this is not true. Dramatic interpretation can be quite exhilarating and rewarding. In addition to the accolades you will receive about your interpretive abilities, you may also begin to understand more about human nature and develop a stronger compassion for your fellow man for you have "walked in his shoes."

Dramatic interpretation is usually defined as a memorized presentation concerning a serious or dramatic subject and is presented with limited movement. Selections are taken from published works and no stage properties or costumes can be used.

If you have decided dramatic interpretation is the competitive event for you, let's discuss preparation for your first competition.

SELECTION

Your selection process should be completed with utmost care and planning. Too many times students see a movie, play or even another forensic student perform and immediately decide "that is the dramatic interpretation for me." Perhaps it will be, but careful analysis of the selection and your abilities should take place before your final selection decision. Considerations should include: selection length, material appropriateness, number and gender of characters, climactic build, your personal abilities and most importantly your attitude about your selection. Do you like the selection enough to live with it for several months?

Enough stress cannot be given to watching movies and plays and to reading plays. Rarely can a coach with several students competing in dramatic interpretation select pieces for everyone that will fit the abilities and personal likes of the competitors. You can be a tremendous help by reading and sharing information about plays with your coach. Much more can be discovered if two people are searching rather than just the coach. It is to your advantage to spend time during the summer reading and researching new material for competition in the fall.

As a novice, you might wonder — "Where do I start in my search for a selection?" Ask friends about their favorite plays. Ask students who have competed previously for selection suggestions. Ask drama and English teachers for ideas and of course, discuss this with your coach. Many times coaches have a file of cuttings or lists of titles appropriate for dramatic interpretation presentation. A short annotated list of selections which have been successfully used in competition is included at the end of this chapter. Your coach can purchase a list of interpretation titles that have been used at the national competitive level. If you are still without a possible selection, skim through play publishing company catalogues; they will include a brief summary of plays. Be careful, however, sometimes the synopsis is much better than the play. A list of play publishing companies and addresses is located in Appendix D. Many times, if your coach does not already have the catalogue, he or she can order one for the school. Remember that you will usually have a more thorough understanding of the play if you can find someone who has read it, rather than a written synopsis.

After obtaining several suggestions, find the scripts and read each entire play. Discuss these plays with someone whose dramatic opinion you respect. It can be another student, your coach, or a drama teacher. What is their opinion of the plot, the characters and especially the dramatic empathic (audience emotional response) potential? After discussion and analysis, choose a play that you particularly like and one that you feel has dramatic potential for you.

Locate a section of the play that has climactic build. These sections must produce a strong empathic response from the listener. Choose a scene that makes you or your friends feel sad, fear, remorse, guilt or anger. If the scene doesn't draw an empathic response, keep searching. Examples include emotional scenes such as a confrontation, a death, or a parting of friends, family or lovers. If you are familiar with *A Raisin in the Sun*, a highly emotional scene occurs when Mama confronts Walter Lee about his wife's intention to abort their baby, or in *A Shayna Maidel* when Rose hears a letter from her mother, that was written shortly before her mother went to the gas chamber during World War II.

Second, consider the dominant gender of the scene's characters. This is not to say a male cannot play a believable female character or vice-versa, but it is more difficult especially for the beginning interpreter. When you attempt to play more than one character from the opposite sex, you are really challenging your abilities. In dramatic interpretation, for the most part, the characters should appear real, like your neighbors and friends, not some wild, zany, unbelievable character that one often sees in humorous interpretation. Exceptions, of course, do exist. *House of Blue Leaves* by John Guare is filled with unusual characters who are set in a bizarre, alarming and pathetically sad situation.

After you have selected the section of the play or book you may wish to use, time it as you read it aloud with emotional expression and dramatic pauses. Realize that your final product may not be the same as this preliminary timing, but you must get an idea of the approximate length of your selection. If the selection is short, let's say, six minutes for a ten minute time limit event, go back to the play and examine areas that could be added. If nothing can be added, perhaps another selection should be considered. Many judges believe you are not competitive if you do not use most of your allowed time. You will be able to add some time with an introduction and through developed dramatic pauses, but try to start with a basic selection of ample time. Talk to your coach about the minimum time you should have. In addition, if your selection is too long, make deletions now, before you waste time memorizing more than you can use.

Making deletions in a selection is a delicate area because most authors do not want their work changed in any way. In addition, some competitive rules indicate certain restraints on cutting or altering a selection. Your coach is your best guide to this decision..

Selections can be tightened up by removing material that doesn't advance the drama. When considering deletions, read your entire selection several times. Mark the material that is absolutely necessary to tell the story or obtain the emotion wanted. Next remove the material that is unnecessary. Can wordage be eliminated by using facial expression or movement? Reread your remaining text and time it. Ask someone who does not know the material to read it with the changes. Does it make sense? Do they follow the story and understand the characters and their motivation? If not, reclaim some of the deleted material.

Sometimes entire characters who do not play a necessary role in the scene are deleted. Sometimes the important lines of an unimportant character are given to one of the major characters, thereby limiting the number of characters to develop. All of this must be done with permission and guidance from your coach.

Many times a selection will piece together two scenes from the same play. Occasionally you will find a short introductory scene early in the play and then perhaps the dramatic climax toward the end. Neither scene is long enough for individual presentation nor are they fully developed separately. When you choose to combine these, you must write a transition to bridge the selections together. It should be done in narrative style to separate it from the actual published selection. Although multiple selections can be successful, one continuous scene is usually preferable.

Before further preparation, the competitor needs to meet briefly with the coach about the chosen selection. The coach can tell you if it is worthy of competition and if the selection is too frequently used. Try to avoid selections that are habitually used year after year. When a contestant walks into a round of competition, and announces the selection, and then hears a negative response such as a heavy sigh or sees a disinterested shift of sitting position, the judge could be non-verbally expressing that this selection is too frequently used. When this occurs the contestant also opens the door to comparison judging. The judge may compare your work to presentations seen before. You don't want to compete with a contestant who isn't even present. Once again exceptions can be made. Choosing to use a popular cutting from *Anastasia* can provide a pleasant surprise to the judge by using a slight accent, stately movement and capturing a wonderful sense of dramatic timing. A performance of a frequently used selection can be refreshing if you have something new and dynamic to offer. In addition don't copy a movie performance. Part of your responsibility as a dramatic interpreter is as a creator not as an impersonator.

The coach should also review dramatic interpretation state and national rules with you before you begin rehearsals. Sometimes these rules differ from contest to contest and you must be able to make adjustments with your selection and performances. Also a contestant does not want to be disqualified because a chair is used or a monologue is used if the rules do not permit. Some rules indicate that a selection must be a multiple character selection; other rules may only suggest it. Some coaches feel that a judge is going to be more impressed by a multi-character selection (if it is done well) because the student has several characters to define, analyze and develop rather than working with just one character. However, if a monologue is developed with extreme care, it too, can impress a judge. Performing a monologue about an old man going fishing does not seem to be highly dramatic, yet it can be spellbinding by capturing an octogenarian in daily habits and gestures. Perhaps multiple character selections are not your forté. With this in mind, remember to select what you do best according to allowable rules. **Clear Glass Marbles, In the Sign** and **My Son, Suzie** are examples of strong, competitive monologues. Novices with little theatrical background should start with a monologue because a single character selection can be developed and polished in a year's work.

Coaches may also discuss the appropriateness of your selection. Will your selection be considered objectionable in competition? Depending upon your area of residence, (some communities are much more conservative than others), a contestant must consider appropriateness of material. If your coach asks you to perform your selection to forensic parents, to the board of education, to the principal or to citizens of the community could you do so without hesitancy? Would you be proud of your selection and performance? Ask yourself, "Could I perform this to my boyfriend's parents or to my grandmother without embarrassment or uneasiness?" If the answer is no, then perhaps you should consider another selection for performance. A selection should never make you uncomfortable. Many totally unobjectionable but wonderful selections exist. Most publishing companies allow deletions of foul language; however, three authors refuse any changes whatsoever to their work: Edward Albee, Tennesee Williams and Samuel Beckett. When in doubt about your selection choice, take your coach's advice, remembering that you are an extension of the forensic program and represent the school in addition to yourself. If the coach asks you to refrain from a particular selection or from offensive language in a selection, then follow his or her judgment.

A contestant must also consider personal performance strengths when selecting competition material. Ask others, including your coach, what they think your strengths are. Do you play senior citizens well? If so, perhaps **The Autobiography of Miss Jane Pittman, Driving Miss Daisy** or **Having Our Say** would be a good selection for you. Maybe you play characters with strength well, so scenes from **Ghosts, I Never Saw Another Butterfly** or *Lion in Winter* would be successful for you. Choose what you do well and continue to develop these abilities.

Your last and extremely important decision to be considered in the selection process is, "Do I love this selection?" Remember that you will be working on this selection for months. The process of practice, refinement and polish ends only with the season's final contest. Never say "I'm so tired of this cutting." Keep looking for ways to improve the performance. If you talk about how tired you are of your work, that attitude will be revealed in competition. Although you are not a professional actor, keep in mind that they must overcome monotony in performance, because they sometimes play a show eight times a week for over a year. They can't get tired of it. It must look fresh and new each time it is performed and so must you in competition.

When you are completely satisfied with your selection, then you are ready to start your rehearsals.

REHEARSAL

Your first obligation in rehearsal is to memorize quickly. Some people prefer to memorize their selection and then work on other elements of performance. Others prefer to work on everything all at once. It doesn't matter which you choose but the first aspect is to get the selection memorized quickly. Many methods of memorization exist. You must decide what works best for you.

METHODS OF MEMORIZATION

1. Say the selection over and over. Try segments at a time. Say the first half page as you look at the script. Try to repeat the half page without looking at it. Repeat until you have that half page memorized.

2. Look at a character's first lines. Think about why he is saying that line. (Some call this subtexting, undertexting, or motivational texting.) Read the line understanding why the character said the line. Cover the line from sight. Repeat the line using your memory of why he said that line. Continue throughout the script going back every five to ten lines to review.

3. Some people tape record the lines and then listen or speak the lines with the recorder. (This could be done as you get ready for school.)

4. Write your cue lines on index cards with your lines on the reverse side. Make sure they are in order.

Other methods exist but whatever your method, memorize your selection as quickly as possible and learn your lines word for word. You must be fair to the author.

Overlearn your lines. Many students who say they are memorized temporarily forget when performing. You don't want this to happen to you at a tournament.

CHARACTER DEVELOPMENT

Next, analyze your characters. Who are they? What are their motives? What are their likes and dislikes? You discover the answers to these questions through analysis of the written and unwritten text. When examining the text, three areas need to be noted: what the character says about himself, what other characters say about the character and what the playwright provides (usually in italics). This is called **text analysis**. What we read between the lines is **sub-text**.

Sarah – I just feel so tired all the time. I can't seem to get everything done. (She plops down on the sofa.)

Text analysis: Sarah has much to do, but because she is tired, she never feels she gets all that she wants to do completed. Sub-text analysis: We conclude that she is *frustrated* because she has too many things to do and not enough time to do them. Key words to consider are *tired* and *plops*. The interpreter might consider delivering her lines with a slower rate and with seeming effort or a small sigh.

Mary – Perhaps you should take some time for yourself for a change. There are other volunteers. Saint Sarah could be shortening her own life.

Text analysis: Mary tells us about Sarah. Sarah thinks of others; she is considerate and generous. To some she may seem saintly.

Sarah – I know there are others who will do this work, but Mary you don't understand the satisfaction- the fulfillment it gives me to help others, while I can.

Text analysis: Sarah feels good about being able to help others. The words *while I can* is a premonition of what is about to be revealed.

Mary – I just know what it's doing to you both physically and mentally. Each time one of the patients die you go through a tremendous turmoil. You don't eat or sleep.

Text analysis: Sarah suffers along with the patients. She appears to have difficulty handling death. Her emotional state after a death affects her physical state and this is harming Sarah's own life.

Sarah – Oh stop! You're exaggerating everything. (Sarah starts to get up from the sofa but doesn't seem to have enough strength. A brief sense of fear crosses her face. She tries again. This time she is successful and starts for the bedroom.)

Text analysis: Sarah brushes it off. The author provides reinforcement of the fact that Sarah is wearing down. It also shows us through her facial expression that she knows she is ill and should slow down but won't. Key words: *strength* and *fear*.

Mary – Sarah, listen to me. It's time you realize you can't do everything and you can't be everyone and you can't be everywhere. It's time you slow down. The doctor has said that you need sometime for yourself before....

Text analysis: Mary feels Sarah tries to do everything for everyone. She needs to reduce her activities and think of herself. Sub-text analysis: Mary implies that Sarah is ill. Key words: *slow down* and *doctor*.

Sarah – Before what? Before I die. (Angry at her sister.) Don't keep reminding me. (Calming down.) My

> work is a way to forget. Mary, you have no comprehension of what a doctor's verdict of terminal illness does to a person. I know you're trying to help and you do this out of love for me but please love what I do for myself because this volunteer work is more for me than for them.
>
> *Text analysis:* Sarah doesn't want to face death. She becomes angry. We also see that they are sisters. Sarah isn't angry at her sister, because she knows that Mary cares for her. Sub-text analysis: Sarah loves her sister, but needs to handle this in her own way.

Next, write three descriptive sentences about Sarah:

- Sarah is **outwardly strong** in facing her terminal illness, but *inwardly afraid.*

- Sarah's **kindness** is shown by taking care of others before taking care of herself.

- Sarah **understands** her sister's concern for her but needs to face death in her own way.

[This is the foundation to the characterization of Sarah.]

After you have studied your script through text and sub-text analysis, write three descriptive sentences about each of your characters.

Now that you have formed characterization foundations, you must decide how you can help the audience visualize these characters because they have no script to follow. You do this in three ways: voice, stance, and focal points.

CHARACTER DEVELOPMENT — VOICE

Each character you portray must have a distinct **voice**. Listen carefully in the classroom before class begins to all the different distinct voices of your fellow classmates. You must provide the audience and judge with such unique and distinct voice qualities so they can follow the selection even when their eyes are not on you (for instance when a judge is writing "excellent" on your ballot). You create voice distinction in two basic ways: **pitch** and **pace**. Pitch is the highness or lowness on a musical scale and pace is the rate of the individual's delivery.

Decide which characters should be in the higher part of your range (usually two or three steps up on a musical scale) and which would fit in your natural range (usually the character with the most lines) and those who might fall into your lower range. Never force yourself into an uncomfortable low or high area or you may be hoarse by the end of the contest and could do damage to your voice. Because you select a predominate range area for each character, it does not mean you are to deliver each character in a **monotone** (repetition of the same pitch). Within each character's range, the use of **inflection** (rise or fall of pitch) must occur or you will be monotonous and boring to your audience.

If your lower range which you had hoped to use for a specific character feels uncomfortable or sounds artificial, place that character in your middle range and then use the second voice element to distinguish one character from another—rate. Listen once again to those classmates before class. This time concentrate on the rate of delivery. Not everyone speaks at the same tempo. If you have two characters in the same pitch, distinguish them by pace or the rate of the delivery of lines. This can get extremely technical and specific, especially if there are several characters in the selection. In dramatic interpretation the characters must sound realistic and therefore a selection with fewer characters (two to five) could be an advantage to you.

Sometimes developing a voice rate can be difficult. Listen to others speak. Can you tap out a pace? Of course there are variances for thought or emphasis but normally we all have a unique pace of our own. Think back to that teacher who went so slowly in her lectures that you were miles ahead of her or the one who went so quickly you could barely get notes down.

Another voice distinction although one not to be overused because it can become artificial, is volume. Strong authoritarian characters such as Amanda in *The Glass Menagerie* would have more force or volume than her shy, almost reclusive daughter, Laura, whose voice would be soft and gentle.

Through pitch, rate and volume, the voice will help the judge visualize (or distinguish) character. Ask a friend and your coach to close their eyes while you perform. Can they tell a difference only through voice? They should be able to hear a distinction. They should be able to tell you the number of characters and each character's personality only through the use of your voice.

CHARACTER DEVELOPMENT — Stance

Character differentiation must also be shown through a character's **stance**. Stance means the way a person stands, his or her posture. Observe how people stand in the hallway or the lunch line. Notice how older people stand compared to younger. Usually an older person's shoulders lean forward and inward toward the center of the body. A typical younger person stands erect, shoulders back and head up. Some people stand with their weight distributed on the balls of their feet; some distribute the weight on the heels while others put most of the weight on one leg. Some people lead with the hips, others with the chest, still others with the head. If you haven't taken an acting class, enroll in one; you will learn many of these basic acting elements. If that does not work into your schedule, borrow an acting book from the drama teacher and study the chapters on characterization, movement and voice.

For each character in your selection develop his/her own stance and each time that character speaks, you must shift to that stance. Check your decisions in front of a full length mirror. Ask other students or your coach to watch your stance shift. Can they tell the type of character by stance? If not, what would they suggest you alter or add? In the following pictures, notice the distinction created by stance:

CHARACTER DEVELOPMENT - Focal Points

The third area that must be addressed for character distinction is focal points. Focal points are specific areas of visual direction. A distinct area must be established for each character in your selection. Let's say your selection has three characters. Your major character would probably be positioned to look toward the center of the room, perhaps looking just to the left of the center judge. Each time that character speaks, you would look at that spot. Sometimes contestants will pick a picture, poster or crack on the wall in that area to have a specific focal point. Make sure you consider the age or size of your character speaking. Many contestants look up as if they are talking to an eight foot person. Your second character might be placed to the left of that focal point at a thirty degree to forty-five degree angle but not a ninety degree angle. A ninety degree angle gives the judge a profile shot of all facial expression and loses half of those expressions. Your third character will then be at a thirty degree to forty-five degree angle to the right. These focal points help the judge distinguish the different characters and you must not mix them up. If you have selected a monologue and that character is talking to several people (a crowd), use the entire audience. Remember also that within our sight angle, some variety should exist: perhaps, the character glances at the floor because he or she can't face the person being addressed or glances down in a time of reflection. Practice your character focal point shifts so they come quickly and correctly.

In review, you have three required basic areas of character delineation that must be developed to assist the judge: voice, stance and focal points. After you are memorized and are performing your selection utilizing these three areas of character delineation, you must continue to refine your presentation by considering personal business, facial expression and the use of dramatic timing.

PRESENTATION REFINEMENT - Personal Business

Personal business in a dramatic interpretation refers to what the characters do with their hands. Are they the type of characters who talk with their hands? Is the character bold, utilizing large gestures full of strength? Is the character shy? What could my hands do to show shyness other than the overused clasped hands? Is the character nervous? Referring back to your three line characterization that you wrote, develop several gestures or personal business for each character. If all of your characters turn a page in a book, each should have a distinguishing way of turning the page-unlike each other. Your best source of ideas for personal business development is observation. Watch the gestures of your parents, teachers and friends. Observe characters in movies and television.

Practice your personal business (gestures) in front of a mirror so it seems natural. Place gestures at certain points in your selection. Some coaches will disagree. Please follow the advice of your coach, so you can adapt to the judging preferences in your area.

Can you walk during your presentation? While walking to change characters is usually not wise, it is possible to insert some movement while in a lengthy speech of one character. This is a question to discuss with your coach who will provide the best source of information and will check specific tournament rules for you.

PRESENTATION REFINEMENT - FACIAL EXPRESSION

In front of a mirror watch your character's face. Is this a happy character? The facial expression for a happy person is quite different from a depressed person. When working with facial expression, remember the eyes are the most expressive part of the face, followed closely by the mouth. Make sure the audience can see your eyes - that means your eyebrows too. Push your hair off your eyebrows for the competition.

Locate pictures of people in magazines such as *People, Newsweek, Time*. Without looking at the message beneath the picture, decide the mood of the person in the picture. Then examine closely the eyebrows and mouth. These should be the elements that tell you how or what that person is feeling. (Glamour magazines won't work well, because most of the people are models who are constantly smiling.)

Work your selection in front of a mirror watching your facial expression. Too many dramatic interpretation presentations feature students with wonderful voice interpretation (pitch, rate, pause, inflection) but no change in facial expression. This must all work together. Sometimes students feel awkward thinking they are overdoing facial expression. For the most part, the opposite is true. Ask your coach if you are overdoing it.

PRESENTATION REFINEMENT - DRAMATIC TIMING

Another area of refinement especially important is dramatic timing which involves the use of pause. Many times students are uncomfortable with silence and they rush into the next speech when what the presentation needs is some "thinking" or "realization" time. Would a pregnant pause intensify the drama at this point? Review the text analysis of your selection. Mark your script where a longer time between words or speeches would add to the dramatic feeling. Practice it until you do not feel uncomfortable with a slice of silence, but remember that during that pause or moment of silence, you still must have facial expression denoting the mood of the character-why the character is pausing.

Slow character switches will cause the performance to drag. You must repeatedly practice the changes from one character to another. Although these changes do not need to move as rapidly as a humorous interpretation, they still must move smoothly and swiftly. Distinct delineation in character changes is required. When one character runs into another (maybe voice of one and stance of another) the performance has "**character blending**." You absolutely should not have character blending in a winning presentation. When one characteristic switches out, so should all the other characteristics for that role and it should happen *at the same time*. This is a difficult element of dramatic interpretation for novice interpreters and it does take hours of work to refine it. Don't get discouraged, you will prevail and succeed.

As you make your character switches, remember a basic element of acting: reacting. Characters must react to the others. All characters must consider what has been said to them, about them, about others, or about a situation and then *react*.

DIALECTS

When using dialects and accents, it is often better to do too little than too much. The judge must understand the dialogue to follow the conflict. If the accent (German, Cockney, etc.) you choose to use is too heavy, the judge may not be able to understand you. Understanding is the key to winning, so don't penalize yourself. Don't add an accent where it is not needed in the script. Humorous interpreters can add accents easily but usually dramatic interpreters stay with what the author has provided in explained characterizations (usually the italics).

An amusing and true story highlights the fact that you should be careful with heavy accents. Foreign exchange students are often on our squad, and one year we selected a play about Germany for a German exchange student. One of the comments on her ballot was "Drop the accent. It doesn't sound real." Many of your judges don't know dialects and accents, but think they do. This can be a problem for the contestant who has spent hours perfecting a natural accent.

PREPARING AN INTRODUCTION

After memorizing, developing character traits (voice and stance), establishing focal points, incorporating dramatic pauses and perfecting character switches, it is time to write an introduction. Keep in mind that the introduction is the first time the audience has heard anything from you and they still have the previous contestant's performance on their minds. Your job is to steal their attention to you and keep it throughout your performance. Because your preceding competitor may have had a powerful selection and performance, you must have something in your first few words to capture the audience's attention. What can you do?

You could pull a few extremely dramatic lines from the play and begin as a character from the play, followed by an explanation in your own words about the characters and the play. Be sure to mention the title and author in the introduction.

Some people start by singing a few lines from a lullaby to introduce a scene about the death of a child or by singing a line or two from a gospel number to introduce a selection of family disintegration.

Excellent creative writers can describe the play or the agony of the characters in their own captivating words which immediately sets the tone or mood of the scene. Sometimes shocking statements, analogies or quotes from the author are used to grab the attention of the judge.

FINAL PREPARATION

Your final step is to practice, practice and practice. Honestly, you can't get enough practice in a three to four month time period for critical competition. The most successful performers are those who know they can't get enough time to practice; those who use all available time to polish and perfect; those who are constantly reexamining and improving their performance level. Don't make your coach force you to practice. If this is necessary, perhaps you are in the wrong event. You must love what you do and take every opportunity to perform and practice. During your practice periods, time your selection making sure you are within the competition time limits. You may need to make adjustments.

A good basic suggestion is to practice alone at first. Sometimes a friend can help with a section but don't force someone to sit through the beginning practices where character development, memorization and stage business are stumbled through. When you have a good feel for your presentation, then ask some fellow forensic student or coach to watch and critique.

The day of competition you should run through your presentation before each round. Find an empty hall or if it's nice, go outside. Practice to a pole, a wall or a locker. Concentrate and do not let anyone disturb you. Running through your performance before you walk into a round helps get the adrenaline flowing and starts setting the mood for you.

AFTER YOUR FIRST COMPETITION

Read your ballots carefully. Don't get angry at your judges; this is how they saw it. Consider the fact that you may have other judges in the future with the same opinion. Do you need to alter something or refine the distinction more to avoid confusion? Rarely, if ever, is a judge "out to get you." Discuss your ballot with your coach. What little changes could you make to clarify a constructive comment. Sometimes it is difficult to think this, but if we had no judges to listen and critique, students would have no competition to attend. Be grateful for every judge who volunteers. Occasionally you will draw a judge who knows little about the event. Comments on your ballot will indicate his lack of knowledge. Realize that five or six others in that round are working under the same circumstances. Can you still come out with the best rank? Keep this in mind when you plan your invitational tournament. Make sure your volunteer judges are briefed on the events they will judge.

REVIEW

TOP NINE TIPS FOR SUCCESS IN DRAMATIC INTERP

1. Know state and NFL dramatic interpretation rules and regulations.

2. Make a wise selection decision that highlights your performance attributes.

3. Memorize quickly.

4. Develop characterization distinction through voice, stance and focal points.

5. Refine your presentation through personal business, facial expression and dramatic timing.

6. Write an introduction.

7. Time your selection.

8. Practice.

9. Study your ballots carefully after every competition.

ACTIVITIES

1. Prepare a distinct stance for these characters:

○ an old professor   ○ a beauty contestant
○ an arrogant politician   ○ a proud cowboy
○ a tired salesman   ○ a frightened teen
○ a "cool" teen   ○ a typical teen

2. Locate ten magazine pictures of people that show distinct stances. Make a collage and label the attitude or mood of each stance.

3. Create distinct personal stage business for the following:

Coughing — as a(n); old person | young child | sophisticated person | ill person

Pointing — with enthusiasm | in fear | with doubt | in confusion | with conviction

Crossing Arms — in defiance | in boredom | in fear | in questioning

4. Read a line from this text varying the rate of delivery to show:

○ irritation   ○ illness   ○ excitement   ○ anger
○ confusion   ○ fear   ○ intelligence   ○ boredom

5. Use inflection to denote meaning with these words or phrases:

"Rain" — as anger | surprise | disbelief | happiness

"I didn't do it" — in anger | surprise | happiness

"Hooray" — in anger | surprise | happiness

6. Use only facial expression to show (do not make any sounds):

○ happiness   ○ questioning (who me?)   ○ anger

○ sadness   ○ surprise   ○ indecision

○ fear   ○ disgust

7. Listen to recordings of poetry, literature or old radio programs to *hear* character differences.

8. Tape record your presentation. Can you *hear* a difference in your characters?

Plays To Consider
For Dramatic Interpretation

Agnes of God - John Pielmeier. Three women. A young nun is accused of murdering her own baby and a psychiatrist is appointed to determine the young nun's sanity.

All My Sons - Arthur Miller. Two men. A father is guilty of making faulty airplane parts for war planes. After being reported missing, his son returns from the war to confront his guilty father.

Amen Corner - James Baldwin. One man and one woman. Mother and son disagree on how he should use his musical talents. She wants him to remain involved with church music while he wishes to leave to perform in jazz joints like his father who left the two of them.

The Boys Next Door - Tom Griffen. Several men. Contains both wonderful serious and humorous material for men. Four mentally handicapped men under the supervision of a social worker are shown confronting daily difficulties that normal people take for granted.

Diviners - Jim Leonard. Two men. A disturbed boy is befriended by a preacher. When the boy was young, he almost drowned in a river and this has left him afraid of water. The minister tries to help him overcome this fear but the result is disastrous.

Dr. Faustus - Christopher Marlowe. Two men. A man makes a pact with the devil and eventually loses his soul to him..

The Effect of Gamma Rays on Man-in-the-Moon Marigolds. Paul Zindel. Two or three women. A story of a widow who bitterly takes out her hopeless situation on her two daughters.

Eleemosynary - Lee Blessing. Three female. Grandmother, mother, and daughter. Alienation of each daughter with her mother create a powerful story.

The Elephant Man - Bernard Pomerance. Two men or one man and one woman. A true story of a man who is hideously deformed.

A Few Good Men - Aaron Sorkin. Two men. A trial of two Marines for their part in the death of another Marine. They are willing to go to jail to uphold the Marine honor code.

Haiku - Katherine Snodgrass. Three women. A mother has two daughters and one of the daughters is labeled "retarded". This daughter remains at home. At times this daughter becomes "super-normal" and creates beautiful poetry.

Home Front - James Duff. Two men. A strong piece for men. A Vietnam veteran relives his trauma substituting his father as the enemy.

I Never Sang For My Father. Robert Anderson. Two men. A challenging scene for a man. The alienation between father and son is apparent throughout this entire show.

I Never Saw Another Butterfly - Celeste Raspanti. Two women or one woman and one man. A Young Jewish girl separated from her family, grows to a young woman in Terezin, a World War II concentration camp.

Little Moon of Alban - James Costigan. One man and one woman. An Irish woman about to be married loses her fiancé from a stray bullet during the Black and Tan disturbances.

Madame Butterfly - Belasco and Long. One woman and one man. A young Japanese woman waits for the return of her child's father - a married American soldier.

A Man For All Seasons - Robert Bolt. Two men. Sir Thomas More, the Lord Chancellor of England, refuses to sign an Act of Supremacy which would make King Henry VIII the spiritual leader of England. King Henry is trying to obtain a divorce from Catherine to marry another woman.

Playing For Time - Arthur Miller. Several women. Women confined to a Jewish concentration camp who save their lives by providing orchestral concerts for the camp commanders.

A Raisin in the Sun - Lorraine Hansberry. Contains several possible scenes for both male and female. A Black family in the 1950s has hopes and dreams of self-improvement in a racist society.

CHAPTER 7

Humorous Interpretation

. . . .

After completing this chapter you should be able to:

❏ Recognize basic styles of humorous interpretation

❏ Choose a selection fitting your abilities

❏ Develop character distinctions through voice, stance, and focal points

❏ Utilize a variety of rehearsal techniques

❏ Introduce personal business and action into the scene in addition to what the script suggests

. . . .

New Terms To Learn In This Chapter

Character Humorous Interpretation

Script Humorous Interpretation

Exaggerated Character

Incongruity

"I think I'll do humorous interpretation because it's so fun! Did you hear all the laughter in the room? It was great!"

HUMOROUS INTERPRETATON

Humorous interpretation can be extremely rewarding for a contestant because of the audience response (laughter) during a performance; however, it requires an acute sense of comic timing, an individual who is extremely comfortable in front of an audience and one who is creative and unabashed by some of the strange voices, stances, and personal stage business that must be performed. If this sounds like you, then let's get started!

Humorous interpretation is frequently defined as a memorized presentation with a comic or entertaining subject that is presented with limited movement. Selections are taken from published works and no stage properties or costumes can be used. Emphasis should be placed on voice and facial expression, and any narrative in the selection should be delivered with energy and animation. Ask your coach to see the specific rules for your state, league and NFL (if you are a member). Always know the guidelines of your event and begin your search for a selection within those perimeters.

With dramatic interpretation contestants should limit the number of characters in their selection because characters need a realistic quality. Humorous interpretation is quite different. Students have performed a multitude of unique characters in their successful performances. What fun it is for the audience to watch the zany character creations. Keep in mind that your selection choice should follow your personality and abilities in comic timing.

Two basic types of humorous selections exist: **character** or **script**. Characterization comedy relies on the establishment of several distinct, creative, usually exaggerated characters in a selection. Humorous lines are in the script, but the audience remembers and laughs more at the "characters" in the scene than what they have to say. Many times the story lines are contrived. Examples of this type of humorous interpretation include: *Cinderella Wore Combat Boots, A Funny Thing Happened on the Way to the Forum, The Perils of Lulu* and *Greater Tuna*. With this type of comic selection, the contestant cannot be shy and afraid to exaggerate. He or she must go to extremes when developing the slow talking, bowlegged, tobacco spitting cowboy or the nerdish prince who is so shy he almost hides from himself. The second type of humorous interpretation is that of a solid comically written script... the lines are important and the characters tend to be more realistic. Although once again characters will need to be developed, the main emphasis is now on comic timing, facial expression, and correct interpretation and delivery of the lines. *The Gin Game*, and *I'm Herbert* are examples of "script" humorous interpretations.

You and your coach must discuss the type of comedy you do best and then search for a selection of that type. Don't rush selecting the correct piece for your abilities. Read and see as many plays as possible. You'll have fun doing this research. Confer with friends, teachers and fellow forensic students about scripts they find humorous. Check with your coach for titles and cuttings that have potential for you. Please refer to the "SELECTION" section in the Chapter Six [Chapter 6, p.94]. This section will assist you in choosing and cutting your selection.

REHEARSAL

If you have selected a play with emphasis on funny characters, you will definitely need to develop unique characters through voice, stance, focal points (where you focus your eyes for each character) and personal stage business. It would be wise to refer to Chapter Six on Dramatic Interpretation for developing characterizations. You will find useful information for this event in this chapter. Explanations with examples are used. After referring to this section of the book, analyze your selection and jot down characteristics for each part. i.e.:

Emily — a shy, wallflower who has low self-esteem
Todd — an athletic, overly proud teen who can't stop talking about himself
John — a conservative, a bookworm fond of historical literature

Sherry — an energetic, happy cheerleader, who is continually preening

Mrs.
Smith — a stern, elderly teacher who is losing her eyesight and hearing.

After you have written a short word characterization for each role you will play, take a sheet of paper and list the character's name and the following headings:

CHARACTER   STANCE   VOICE   FOCAL POINT   BUSINESS

Now look at your word characterization for the first character, Emily. She is shy, nervous and has low self-esteem. What exaggerated characteristics could you develop for her to give her humor in your selection? Perhaps she would stand with shoulders in and her head somewhat down. She might be pigeon-toed. She might lift her head somewhat to say her lines and then the head would go back down because she would not be able to look at anyone in the eye; she is too shy. To show nervousness, she could fidget with her hair or fingers or imaginary clothing. She might jiggle her leg a little in nervousness. Her voice could be softer and perhaps a bit squeaky which would help illustrate her low self-esteem. Know anyone like this? Probably not, because  we have taken this character to the extreme. We have **exaggerated** her characteristics. Comedy will usually have exaggeration or **incongruity** embedded somewhere. Now fill out the chart.

CHARACTER	STANCE	VOICE	FOCAL POINT	BUSINESS
Emily	shoulders in leaning in knees together	soft but, squeaky	minor character 45 degrees to left of center	fidget with clothing, hair, fingers, jiggle leg

Take your next character, Todd, and think through the same headings as you look at your simple word characterization of him. Then fill in the headings on your character work sheet.

CHARACTER	STANCE	VOICE	FOCAL POINT	BUSINESS
Todd	stand tall	strong	major character	pretending
	chest out	overbearing	barely off center	to throw a
	chin up	grabs		football
		attention		combs hair

After you have analyzed two of your characters, try switching from one to another quickly, that is, change the stance, voice (say a line), focal point and the business. Switch back and forth. You may have to make adjustments on stance and personal stage business to allow the character switch to go smoothly and quickly.

Continue to add a character at a time and develop the voice, stance, focal point and personal stage business for each character. Experiment with movement from one character to another. Can you change characters quickly and distinctly? Do not allow character blending. [Refer to Dramatic Interpretation, Chapter 6, p.102]

Experiment with movement from one character to another.

After you have developed and tested all of your characters, start putting them with the script. Many humorous interpretation contestants memorize first, and as they memorize, experiment a little with characters. So many types of characters, stances, and business exist, that it is often a slow and frustrating process to try to memorize and establish characters at the same time.

After you are memorized and have established characters, work for quick changes between them. If you are too slow between character changes, your comic timing can be thrown off. Usually a humorous interpretation is fast-paced. When students are asked to pick up the pace between characters they invariably pick up the pace of the character's lines. NO! Remember, each character has a certain pitch range and delivery rate. Don't let your quick-paced transitions alter your character delivery rate. Sometimes this is difficult to master but it can be done with concentration and practice.

The second type of humorous interpretation is a script that is so cleverly written that the performer's main thrust of performance is the use of excellent comic timing. Your first step with this type of humorous interpretation is to make sure you understand every line. If you don't, ask someone to explain the humor or the intent of the line. Look up any words that you do not know. Only by knowing the intent of the line or word can you perform the correct timing to the delivery. Many students have trouble setting up the humorous line. Situation comedies on television will illustrate how humor is "set up". Rent videos and listen intently to the "set up" and emphasis on humorous lines. This is what you must do in this type of selection. You do not want to miss a humorous line. If you are performing a selection that is well-known and you are missing that sense of comic timing and "setup", you will be penalized. This is a difficult type of selection, but some people are just naturals. They have the "timing" to be funny. *The Gin Game*, for example, is a funny play, but can be hilarious when performed with perfect comic timing on each line.

The importance of good facial expression cannot be overstressed in a humorous interpretation presentation. On "character" selections, you must be willing to be a clown at some points. Exaggeration is the key to a successful performance with "character" selections. This is especially true with facial expression. Always practice your facial antics in front of a mirror. Get used to the way you look; it *should* be funny.

INTRODUCTIONS

After you have worked your humorous interpretation and it is coming along well, start thinking about how you will introduce your selection to your judges. This is extremely important; it is the first vocal impression the judge has of you.

Perhaps you will start your performance with about twenty to thirty seconds from the script. This should be captivating and grab attention immediately. Next, give a brief explanation of the scene and characters and always include the name of the selection and the author. Your entire introduction should run between thirty-five seconds and one minute. Anything more gets a little tiring. Work out exactly what you want to say in as few, precise words as possible. Get to the actual script presentation. Practice this introduction diligently so that the first vocal presentation is impressive. What a good way to start! Yes, the introduction is also memorized.

Singing a short segment of "A Comedy Tonight" immediately caught the attention of the audience for one young performer who then gave a brief explanation of his selection: *A Funny Thing Happened On The Way To The Forum*.

If you can think of a clever, imaginative opening, you are off to a good start. Some students compose an introduction in the hallway outside the competition room before they enter the room to compete. Usually these last minute introductions do not work well and seldom impress the judge. Remember the contestant who performed immediately before you still has the judge's attention. You need to steal the attention held by the previous performer and direct it to you.

TOP NINE TIPS FOR SUCCESS IN HUMOROUS INTERP

1. Know state and NFL humorous interpretation rules and regulations.

2. Decide which type of humorous interpretation best suits your personality and abilities.

3. Memorize quickly.

4. Develop characterization distinction through voice, stance and focal points.

5. Refine your presentation through personal stage business, facial expression and comic timing.

6. Rehearse switching from one character to another smoothly and quickly.

7. Write an introduction and memorize it.

8. Time your selection and practice, practice, practice.

9. Study your ballots carefully after every competition.

ACTIVITIES

1. Create five outlandish, exaggerated characters utilizing stance and gestures. Move as quickly as possible into each character as a classmate calls them out. i.e., cowboy, waitress, hairdresser, weightlifter, nerd.

2. Read two paragraphs from a magazine. On each sentence switch your voice, through your five characters.

3. Rent Carol Burnett's television variety show or Red Skelton's television show videos. Watch closely their comical characters — their gestures, facial expression, movement and voice. Notice how the actor/actress has created differences among the characters.

4. Rent comic movies that have been hits. Listen carefully to the delivery of the lines. Notice the sense of comic timing... the line "setup", and the slight pause to highlight or draw attention to a line or reaction. Listen to the use of inflection (rise or fall of the pitch of the voice.)

5. Review the activities for Dramatic Interpretation in Chapter Six. [Chapter 6, p.111]

Plays To Consider
For Humorous Interpretation

Actor's Nightmare - Christopher Durang. George, an accountant, is mistaken for an understudy and is called upon to take the place of an injured actor.

Adaptation - Elaine May. *Adaptation* is a picture of man from birth to death played through a game show.

Baby With the Bathwater- Christopher Durang. Durang's zany characters satirize parenthood.

Blind Date - Horton Foote. A well-meaning aunt tries to play cupid for her obnoxious niece.

Brighton Beach Memoirs- Neil Simon. As a Brooklyn teenager in the 1930s, Simon narrates the story of his life.

Cemetery Club, The - Ivan Menchell. Three Jewish widows meet once a month before visiting their husband's graves.

Cinderella Wore Combat Boots- Jerry Chase. Another version of Cinderella where the regular characters take a delightful twist.

Cyrano de Bergerac - Edmond Rostand. Cyrano, an extraordinary man, satirically looks at his life as he describes his large nose.

Fools- Neil Simon. Leon Tolchinsky, a school teacher lands a job in Kulyenchikov, a village that has been cursed with stupidity.

Foreigner, The - Larry Shue. Charley, who is extremely shy about visiting with strangers, pretends to be a foreigner who is unable to speak English.

Funny Thing Happened on the Way to the Forum, A- Burt Shevelove and Larry Gelbart. Music by Stephen Sondheim. A Roman slave schemes freedom by obtaining a beautiful woman for his young master.

Greater Tuna - Jaston Williams Joe Sears and Ed Howard. A small town of Tuna, Texas is highlighted through their local radio station along with the unusual characters who live there.

Laughing Wild - Christopher Durang. A humorous look at ordinary life in urban America.

Laundry and Bourban - James McClure. Three Texas women as unlike as they can be, gossip about life in a small town.

Lend Me a Tenor- Ken Ludwig. When the real world famous opera tenor takes a double dose of tranquilizers and cannot perform, the general manager dons a costume and performs; however the real singer awakes, puts on his costume and now there are two look-a-like performers.

Little Shop of Horrors- Howard Ashman and Alan Menken. Seymour works in a florist shop which has a talking, human-eating plant.

Nerd, The- Larry Shue. A young man who was saved by a fellow G.I. in Vietnam and has never met him, invites Rick to come for a visit. Rick is a nerd with no social sense and he overstays his welcome.

CHAPTER 8

Prose and Poetry Interpretation

· ·

After completing this chapter you should be able to:

❑ Distinguish between poetry and prose selections

❑ Locate appropriate material for competition

❑ Develop strong characterizations through textual and/or subtextual analysis

❑ Properly use a folder for presentation

❑ Identify movement allowances and restrictions

❑ Explore the use of voice by varying volume, pitch, and rate to express character and mood

· ·

New Terms To Learn In This Chapter

Prose

Script Interpretation

Free Verse

Narrative Prose

"Forensics sure looks fun, but I don't know if I could perform in front of an audience. I get too nervous."

PROSE AND POETRY INTERPRETATION

Have you said or thought that? You need to investigate interpretation of prose (material written in ordinary language without verse or meter) or poetry. This may be the event for you. These events (**prose** and poetry) are sometimes combined in competition but often they are separate event competitions defined as **script interpretation** which means contestants have their scripts (in a folder) before them and they are expected to interpret the selection's characters, mood and meaning through voice, facial expression and gesture. The performance is not to be memorized except for the introduction. Time limits vary according to the state, league or national competition. Once again, check with your coach for the particulars of these events in your area.

If this is your first year in competition and you haven't decided which event to choose or you feel reluctant to compete because of inexperience in speech or theatre, this is an excellent way to get started. Because you have a script before you, some of the memorization fear is eliminated. You only have a short thirty to forty-five second introduction to write and memorize. You can do that! The bulk of your event is typed and contained in a small, three-ring notebook which you have in front of you during your performance. You may and actually should refer to it as you perform.

SELECTION

Another nice feature of prose/poetry interpretation is that the event can be either humorous or dramatic. Dramatic selections seem to be chosen more frequently and often do better in final rounds. Sometimes, a well performed comic prose or poetry selection can be a relief to a judge who has been listening to heavy drama most of the day and is beginning to get depressed by all the terrible events of the world. So, if you find a humorous selection and feel you would do better with it, certainly don't discard it for a more frequently used serious selection. You may have just what the judge needs, and he or she certainly will remember you and your selection.

PROSE SELECTIONS

Prose selections are found in books rather than plays. You may find a wonderful, successful selection from books you have read. Ask teachers who are prolific readers for ideas and ask them what part of the book was their favorite. Dramatic selections should contain conflict that includes difficult and worthy decisions and consequences. Humorous selections should have clever dialogue, incongruity or exaggerations. If you find a section of a book that you believe would be good for dramatic performance or a section that is clever and funny, your next step is to read the entire book. You should always know the complete work because sometimes other sections of the work will give you insight into characters, plot or conflict.

POETRY SELECTIONS

With poetry, visit your school and public library and try to find some new material, if possible. Remember that poetry can be either rhymed or **free verse** (poetry that does not rhyme or has a loose rhyme pattern.) Most students when they first start to look for poetry, search for a rhymed selection, which can be a real problem, when you start working on pace variety. Keep in mind that longer selections seem to appeal and are remembered better after the performance. A story that judges can visualize helps them remember your work. Highly emotional passages are also memorable. If you decide to put several selections together under a theme, showing how different authors look at the same subject, such as "Hate", "War" "Children", "Memories", keep in mind that they are sometimes not as memorable as a plot or story that can be recalled. Whatever you choose, you must love it first, before you can capture the attention of the judge, so choose what *you* want and like. Everyone is different and what works for one student may not work for another.

Be warned about rhymed poetry. Poetry presentations that are too sing-songy are tuned out. The story or idea can be lost in the rhythm; the rhythm should accent the piece but not overshadow the meaning. If you choose a rhymed poem, work especially hard to overcome the temptation to get into a repetitious pace pattern. It becomes similar to little nursery rhymes that are sometimes sung. Pick a nursery rhyme such as Jack and Jill, Mary, Mary Quite Contrary, or Little Bo Peep. As you say the nursery rhyme, clap your hands to the accented words. Notice the repetitious rhythm.

If you have found a selection that you like and it is rhymed, look closely at the punctuation the author has given you. This will help. Don't end the thought or sentence at the end of a line if there is no punctuation to tell you to stop or pause. Continue that thought or phrase until the author tells you what to do through the punctuation provided.

Once again, serious poetry seems to do better in final rounds than the less serious. However, sometimes it is nice to be the winning exception. Humorous poetry is a little more difficult to find, and often works of great poets will not be in this category, but some rhymed poems written for children can be enjoyable. They can be presented in such a delightful way that any judge can't help but score the contestant up there with others who are doing poetry of recognized artists.

Finding new material in poetry is often difficult. It may take you many library searches. Don't give up too easily. Once again, if you can find poetry on your own instead of grabbing one that your coach has used year after year for other students, it will benefit both you and your coach. You will also not be tempted to imitate a performance that was given the year before, and your coach will not be tempted to coach a carbon copy of a previous year.

PROSE AND POETRY PREPARATION

When you begin thinking about your performance, think of a parent reading a bed time story to a son or daughter and all the energy, excitement and versatility used to enhance the words of the story. This is the basis of prose and poetry interpretation. You are telling a story with emotion to your adult audience and you wish their attention, so you do everything possible within the limits of your event rules to grab and hold their attention. It's much more difficult telling a story to an adult especially one who must sit through six or seven at a time. Whereas a child would love to hear six or seven in a row, (it puts off going to bed) the adult audience is ready to do something else. Don't let them nap during your performance! You must captivate and hold your audience's attention for seven minutes (or whatever your time limit is. Be sure to know.)

How do you hold the attention of the audience? You certainly don't want to be like the school teacher who reads a chapter to you from your text-book and almost puts you to sleep. Think back to that situation and what made the presentation so boring? Was it monotone? Was it delivered at the same pace throughout? Was it delivered too slow or too fast? Was anything set off as important? When you compete, you must use variety and be dynamic!

Remember that your event is interpretation of poetry or prose not just reading a selection. As you practice, look at the underlying meaning of the words, or the subtext. You need to "read between the lines" to discover the feeling that the author is trying to convey. Sometimes what the selection says and what it means are not quite the same. The meaning of the line is the subtext. Read through your selection one line at a time and rephrase each line into your own words of meaning — this is a form of subtexting. It is like talking between the lines. An example might be something like this:

[actual line] He called to her in the other room.
[subtext] *He was angry.*

[actual line] "Why isn't supper ready for the children?"
[subtext] *What have you been doing all day? Watching soap operas?*

[actual line] "Sara and Ben deserve more than they are getting from their mother."
[subtext] *I can't believe your attitude toward your children. What has changed you? You used to always put the children first. Now look at them, filthy, hungry...*

[actual line] "What is going on?"
[subtext] *I need an explanation. I'm willing to listen but without an explanation , I may take the children and leave.*

In practice go through your entire script and for each statement create a subtext statement. This will help you develop a reason for the author's lines. Remember that you cannot rewrite, add or delete an author's work. Subtexting is for rehearsal only.

In addition to a subtextual analysis, look closely at the adjectives, adverbs and verbs — the descriptive and action words. For performance, these words need special treatment. Always know the meaning of every word in your selection.

With trepidation he moved slowly and quietly toward the door.

What does trepidation mean? Most people know it means fear, but it also means with a trembling movement. How could the interpreter show a trembling fear? Could he have a hesitation in his delivery? Could he use a slight trembling gesture? How does the interpreter suggest the rate of the movement to the door? Perhaps by reducing the rate of the line delivery or the delivery rate of the single word, "slowly". Another technique is to extend the vowel sound. What could the reader do for "quietly"? Experiment with your adjectives and verbs. Could the performer whisper "quietly"?

Each interpretative selection is like a coloring book which contains only guidelines and your job as an interpreter is to carefully choose your "crayons" (interpretive tools) to create the picture intended by the author.

If you have characters in your selection, create a distinguishable style for each character. This includes pitch, inflection, pace and the use of pause. The judge must be able to hear a difference between characters. Since prose and poetry are judged heavily on voice and facial expression, those are the two areas of utmost concern as you rehearse because judges will be watching your face and listening to your voice. Rehearse in front of a mirror watching closely your facial expression, especially what  your eyes are saying. Without saying a word but by merely a "look", can you show the character's attitude and how it changes? In front of the mirror watch the changes in facial expression as you think (don't speak) the words. Can you see changes on your face or does it stay basically the same? It should not stay the same throughout the selection. Perhaps you could watch a movie with the sound off. Highly dramatic scenes offer great examples of facial expression changes.

Remember that no matter what the words say, they become monotonous when nothing varies. You must use inflection (rising or falling of pitch). Rising inflection denotes questions, disbelief, excitement. Falling inflection denotes, rejection, finality, sadness. Experiment with inflection. Try the activities at the end of the chapter.

You must also work on your timing and the pace of the performance. Locate areas in your selection that are of dramatic importance. How can you highlight them? Consider how pace or pausing might help. Serious works usually have a slower rate with a built-in rate toward the climax.

Don't be afraid to give characters silence... a moment to react and think; especially before some dramatic responsive reply. Let's look at an example of the use of pausing. Take a look at the following prose. Read the selection straight through with pauses only at the end of sentences:

> "Joan, you must make your decision now. We can't wait. Your mother will be fine without you here. Others will help her. They have said they would. We'll never have this opportunity again. Remember, don't let her live her life through you."

> (Turning away and thinking. With great reluctance and hesitation.) "I can't go."

> "Joan, please think of yourself for a change. You have lived your entire life for her. Don't do this."

> "How could I desert her now... at her age... when she most depends on me? I would constantly be wondering if she was okay. You have no idea what life is like being blind. I do, because I was born blind but surgery corrected my eyesight. The condition was too developed to be corrected for her. I am her eyes... her link to the seeing world. To move her from her home, or from me would destroy her. I can't go. I love you dearly but, I love her too. I cannot do this to her."

Yes, a little melodramatic, sorry, but this is just to make an illustration of using the dramatic pause. Now read the same selection again on the following page, this time containing pause marks. / means short pause (a single beat), //means a longer pause (3 or more beats).

"Joan, you must make your decision now. We can't wait. // (assuring her) Your mother will be fine without you. Others will help her. They have said they would. / (another reason) We'll never have this opportunity again. // (Look how she still controls you.) Remember, don't let her live her life through you. What do you say? Will you come with me now?"

//(long pause, perhaps turning away slightly. With great hesitation and reluctance)
"I can't go."

"Joan, please think of yourself for a change. You have lived your entire life for her.. Don't do this."

"How could I desert her now? At her age? ....When she needs me most. How would I live with myself? I would constantly be wondering if she was okay. You have no idea what life is like being blind. I do, because I was born blind, but surgery corrected my eyesight. The condition was too developed to be corrected for her. I am her eyes/ her link to the seeing world. To move her from her home or from me would destroy her. / / (long, thinking pause... a final decision) I can't go. /I love you dearly, / but I love her too. //(long pause of 3 beats... possibly looking down and then up with a definite decision in voice.) I cannot go."

Narrative prose (story without dialogue) must also make use of pausing:

With difficulty Joseph picked up his coat, // looked earnestly at Joan, // gave her a light kiss and walked out of her life forever. /// Joan's mother passed away the following year.

Notice the difference in meaning through just the use of pause. Mark your own script. Be sure to time your selection again after this exercise because with the additional pauses you may exceed your time limits and may need to cut your selection.

Old recordings of plays or poetry for classroom use are excellent examples of inflection, pace and pause. Your English teacher might be able to help you locate some. Old radio recordings, especially the dramas will also be useful.

INTRODUCTIONS

In your thirty to forty-five second introduction, be innovative and creative but don't forget to also inform. The judge and audience need to know something about the story, or a character within the selection or about the author. Choose something that will catch the attention of your audience and lead them into your presentation. Perhaps a reference to the author's confinement to a mental institution and that the work to be presented was begun while she was a patient could be worked into an intriguing introduction to her work. Look up the biography of the author of your selection. You will find many interesting and often unusual information that might be a change of pace from the typical introduction of a character line from the work. Sometimes a well-written philosophical introduction can be quite effective. Remember to be unique. Make sure your introduction includes the name of the selection and the author. It must be memorized and is your first vocal impression to your judge and audience. Impress them!

PREPARING THE FOLDER

Type your prose or poetry selection and place it in your folder. You may want to double space the typing so you can add interpretation notes (stress marking, pause placements, rising inflection on certain words, etc.) to the typewritten script. A small, hardback, three-ring black folder is most commonly used. It is less distracting than someone's school folder with stickers and graffiti all over it. You do not want the judge spending more time trying to read the front of your folder than listening to your performance.

Always practice with your folder. Place your right hand at the bottom right edge with a finger in place behind the page to be turned before it needs to be turned. Never should there be a break in the middle of thought or dialogue while you turn the page. I would suggest that you memorize the last two or three sentences on each page and the first two or three sentences on the next in case of some type of problem that might occur as you turn the page (pages stick together, etc.) Always be ready. Another reason to rehearse with the same script and folder is so that you know where every prose or poetry line is located on the paper. If something should distract you for a moment, (like someone walking into the room during your performance), you will be able to glance down to the exact spot and keep going without becoming disturbed.

Make sure you hold your script low enough and yet away from your body, so we see your facial expression and not the top of your head.

At the conclusion of your presentation don't slap your folder closed. Close it quietly and either sit to hear the next performer or leave unobtrusively. Never comment in front of a judge about your performance. If you didn't feel that you had a good performance, wait until you are out of the judge's hearing to make a comment about your mistakes. Don't plant any ideas!

Even if you did make some mistakes, remember to put that performance behind you. Don't dwell on mistakes. You have a fresh new round with a new judge, so don't bring mistakes from a previous round with you.

MOVEMENT

You are somewhat restricted by the script but most rules still allow minor movement in prose. A curtsy, an outstretched hand, a wiping of your hand on you forehead are typical allowable movements. Walking about or across the room is usually not allowed. Students should stay within the "camera picture" and make sure their movement is in response to the literature and not forced upon it.

> **Carolyn reached out her hand to touch his forehead as she knelt beside him.**
> *[You could extend your hand but to kneel might be considered in the acting category.]*

> **Covering her eyes, as she looked toward the explosion, Mary moved swiftly to the shelter.**
> *[You could look in a specific different direction and perhaps your hand could come up as if to protect your eyes, but you would remain stationary.]*

REHEARSAL

Often students give the excuse that they don't need to rehearse if they can read a script. Wrong! You still need character development, vocal variety, facial expression, dramatic timing, and script familiarity. This does not come without practice. Those students who make the final round have taken this event seriously and have rehearsed as much as students competing in other areas.

This Is A Great Event! Have Fun With It And You Will Experience Success.

REVIEW

TOP NINE TIPS FOR SUCCESS IN POETRY AND PROSE INTERP

1. Know state and NFL prose and poetry rules and regulations.

2. Choose material that will be of interest to an audience.

3. Type your selection and place it in a three ring folder.

4. Practice proper use of the folder in rehearsal.

5. If applicable, develop your characterizations and selection mood.

6. Refine your presentation through facial expression, vocal variety and dramatic timing.

7. Write an introduction.

8. Time your selection and practice.

9. Study your ballots after each contest and make adjustments.

ACTIVITIES:

1. Listen to recordings of radio mystery shows. Listen carefully to the use of inflection, pace and pause.

2. Take a newspaper story and exaggerate the interpretation as you read it aloud. Don't get ludicrous and lose the thrust of this activity.

3. Take a paragraph from a novel and speak the subtext as a fellow classmate reads the paragraph. (You will need to work this out.)

4. Visit a library that has a children's storyteller. Listen to her perform to a group of children.

5. Work up a children's story to read at a grade school. Make sure you exaggerate: facial expression, voices and pauses.

6. Watch fellow classmates as they read stories to young children. Watch the performer but also watch the audience response.

7. Listen to recordings of poetry. Follow the script to see where the interpreter pauses or changes the pace of delivery. Analyze why those interpretive decisions were made. Write the motivational meaning between the lines of your printed script of the recording. Play the recording but read your written motivational meaning.

8. Listen to a live interpretive performance. In larger cities, bookstores will have readings of prose or poetry. Check your local newspaper for such events or call your bookstores to inquire about performances.

9. Turn to the activities section after the Dramatic Interpretation chapter in this book. Many of these activities will also be beneficial to you as you prepare your prose or poetry.

Duet Acting

After completing this chapter you should be able to:

❏ Identify the basic elements of duet acting

❏ Select appropriate material and a compatible partner.

❏ Use the acting chain for realistic performances

❏ Develop blocking that accents the characters and the scene

❏ Create an introduction that is informative and draws attention to the performers

New Terms To Learn In This Chapter

Observation

Blocking

Stage Picture

Motivation

Duet acting is an event especially good for novice forensics students. You will have a partner in performance and you will memorize a scene from a published script. This event varies widely from state to state so be sure you know all the rules regulating duet acting in your area.

Some competition areas allow only chairs as set pieces; some allow any number of chairs but only one table. The combinations are varied so know your specific rules. In some parts of the country actors are allowed to play multiple roles in a scene (similar to a dramatic interpretation) while other rules stipulate each actor can play only one role. As with every event, know the rules!

SELECTION

Perhaps the most challenging aspect of this event is finding an appropriate selection. Sometimes it will be difficult to locate selections that fit within the time limit, fit the abilities of both actors and have equal appeal to both performers. Choose selections that are equally balanced between characters so one performer is not carrying the burden of the presentation. Often two actresses wish to perform together. Finding new material for two women is a challenge.

Sometimes forensics students are asked to sign up for duet acting and then the coach casts the positions as in a play. Students may also be allowed to audition a scene and if it has potential for both performers then they are encouraged to use it in competition.

If you are going to make your own selection, remember when choosing a dramatic scene it should have a climax. Always have a strong conclusion to your scene. If you are not well read in theatre, perhaps you should visit with your coach about possible scenes for presentation. He or she will be able to guide you in your selection.

After making your scene selection, decide who is best suited for each role. Consult your coach before making a final decision. MEMORIZE QUICKLY.

Next, start developing your character. Consider these factors: age, health, attitude, and prosperity. With these characteristics in mind, start developing a stance and walk that illustrates this information about the character.

When preparing a dramatic scene search deep into the play to develop your character. Rarely will you locate scenes for teenage characters. This means that your body stance and personal business will be unlike your natural habits. Always read the entire play for insight into characterization and motivation. For characterization development, list descriptive adjectives that you locate or interpret in script dialogue.

Example:

"Oh she wouldn't hurt a flea."
[kind, caring]

"Even though she's eighty years old, she's up at 6:00 A.M. and out in the barn doing daily chores."
[older lady, healthy]

"I won't have you using the Lord's name in vain in my house."
[strong religious belief]

List those adjectives: **kind, caring, old, healthy, religious**

When you examine an entire play you will have a much longer list which defines your character more precisely.

For the preceding example, observe older people. Go the mall and watch senior citizens as they move, eat or purchase items. Rent a movie such as *Driving Miss Daisy* and observe the body positions, the walks and the personal businesses of these characters.

AN ACTOR MUST BE A KEEN OBSERVER OF LIFE

You must start to observe people around you. What do they do with their hands? How do they stand? These **observations** (noticing and mentally recording facts and events) help you develop traits for your duet characters.

One of the most important elements that must be included in preparing this event is that you must block the movement in the scene. You may need your coach to assist you with this element. **Blocking**, movement that is theatrically correct and develops the scene and characters rather than distract from them, should be an important part of your scene. Always follow basic acting rules when creating movement. If you are not sure of the basic blocking movements, consult an acting textbook. Your coach will be able to share basic, fundamentally correct movements with you as you begin your rehearsals. Examples of basic blocking guidelines include: lead with the upstage foot, cheat open, and cross in front when you have the line. Variety in **stage picture** (the positions of actors on stage) should also be utilized; that is, don't *sit* through the entire scene.

Most judges have trouble judging students in a duet acting event when they apparently don't know or follow basic acting movement rules. After all, the event is duet *acting*. In addition to correct acting movement, remember that all movement must look **motivated** (believable).

TIMING

After you have your blocking and lines memorized start refining your characterization and character relationships. Your timing between character responses comes with practice. Utilize all the practice time you can obtain. Keep in mind that in acting a response is necessary to everything said. The response may be a pause, a raised eyebrow, or a movement. It is not always the next line. Sometimes a silent reaction is necessary before a verbal response to a preceding line. Too many times students rush their lines and reactions. Remember your performance is to appear as if it's the first time you've heard each line: listen and react. Below is an illustration of an acting chain.

1st **speaker** — Talk ⇌ Listen ⇌ React ⇌ Talk ⇌ Listen ⇌ React ⇌ Talk ⇌ Listen ⇌

2nd **speaker** — Listen ⇌ React ⇌ Talk ⇌ Listen ⇌ React ⇌ Talk ⇌ Listen ⇌ React ⇌

INTRODUCTIONS

You are memorized, blocked, motivated, characterized and ready for competition. Well almost. Don't forget that you must introduce your scene. You must be creative, informative and brief. The audience needs to know what happened before your scene and who the two characters are. This is your first impression to the judge and audience and your introduction needs to take the attention away from the preceding performance. Sometimes contestants will start the dialogue of the scene and after about twenty to thirty seconds will freeze and begin an explanation of the scene, the characters, the title and the author. A slight pause separates the introduction from the rest of the selection delivery. Another introductory method is to share the information. An example might be that one character introduces and tells something about the other as the second character is pantomiming an action from the upcoming scene. Then the action character stops to explain the first actor as he/she pantomimes something. Usually both actors say the title and author together to end the introduction. Pause briefly and then begin the scene. Whatever you choose to do for an introduction, always include the title, author, and an explanation of the scene and characters.

In duet acting, movement is important so be sure the clothing that you select to wear does not restrict that element. Ladies need to remember that an extremely short skirt will limit movement. Sitting is awkward. Sit in front of a full length mirror to see if that skirt will work for your scene. What if blocking calls for you to stand on the chair or lie down on the table? Dressing in costume is usually prohibited but if the character in the play would wear a dress then wear a dress. If one of the characters would be in a suit, at least dress up with a tie and perhaps a jacket. This will help the audience visualize the character without a full costume.

In addition, remove any jewelry that might be distracting or with which you might unconsciously fidget during a scene. In reference to the elderly character developed earlier in this chapter, it would be unlikely that she would nervously twist her high school ring. If you are tempted to do this, put the jewelry in a pocket, purse or don't wear it to the tournament.

After competition remember to study your ballots carefully. Discuss the judge's comments with your coach. Decide what you can do to improve your performance. Continue to practice and perfect your scene. Don't let the scene go stagnant.

Break A Leg!

REVIEW

TOP NINE TIPS FOR SUCCESS IN DUET ACTING

1. Know the rule limitations for this event.

2. Wisely select your scene and your partner.

3. Creatively and accurately block your scene

4. Memorize your scene quickly.

5. Develop characters through play analysis and observation.

6. Use the acting chain... Talk... Listen... React

7. Prepare a creative introduction

8. Practice, practice, practice.

9. Study your ballots carefully after each contest.

ACTIVITIES

1. Stand before a full length mirror and create body stances for:

- a tired, elderly man
- a five-year old
- a soldier on duty
- a henpecked husband
- a weightlifter
- a model

2. Interpret these lines.

"He went that a way" (nervous, proud, unsure, matter-of-fact, deceivingly, happy)

"I want my money back." (nervous, proud, unsure, matter-of-fact, deceivingly)

3. Through demonstration, share with the class three characterization observations.

4. Demonstrate each of these actions as these various characters:

ACTIONS:
opening a bottle of catsup   salting your meal
sealing an envelop   blowing up a balloon
breathing with difficulty

CHARACTERS:
a ninety-seven year old   a meticulous lady
a four year old   an egotistical man

5. Study film. Observe the eyes of actors. Watch for reactions through face and body rather than line reactions.

CHAPTER 10

Improvised Duet Acting

· ·

After completing this chapter you should be able to:

❑ Identify the components of improvised duet acting

❑ Present active rather than passive presentations

❑ Understand the importance of regular rehearsals

❑ Use creativity in character development, movement and the use of props

❑ Prepare a creative introduction

New Terms To Learn In This Chapter

Improvise

Action

Conflict

Tag Line

THE INS AND OUTS OF IMPROVISED DUET ACTING

Although this event is not used in all states, it is presented in this book because it can be one of the most challenging, creative and entertaining events at a tournament Currently many coaches do not favor improvised duet acting (IDA) because students are not performing the event as it was meant to be performed. In **improvised**, (composed and performed on the spur of the moment,) duet acting, two contestants choose one topic from a group of several topics. The performers then have thirty minutes to prepare a complete scene which includes an introduction, plot, characterizations, **conflict** and a resolution. Normally the better IDA performers will use all thirty minutes of preparation time knowing that they can improve their performance with each run through of their scene. Contestants may choose to perform either a dramatic or comic scene from the topic they draw. Most contest rules include a minimum time limit and a maximum time limit. Many contests use the four minute minimum and seven minute maximum time limits.

Contestants in this category must be able to think on their feet, create a story and play a variety of characters. The two performers should have a good working relationship and be willing to listen and accept ideas from each other.

In preparation for this event, you and your partner must sit down and discuss characters that each of you can create. Then make a list of each of your original characters. The following is an example of comic character possibilities for two students.

TOM	SARA
Billy Bob—a good ole country boy	Petunia—a shy, nervous wallflower
Hank—a red-neck tobacco chewing thug	Jo—a tough, loud-mouth macho girl
Floyd—a stern right-to-business man	Mitzi—the dumb gum-chewing,
Sam—a smooth-talking, car salesman	secretary

For comic improvised duet acting, work on developing exaggerated characters for possible competition.

For each of these characters that you have listed, develop a stance, a walk, and some stage business. Let's look at the character of Sam, the smooth-talking car salesman. Let's give him some personal business which can be described as habits or movements which help define the character. Perhaps he could use breath spray frequently, slick his hair back, jingle the coins in his pocket and stand with his shoulders back with an arrogant attitude. His talk would be fast and probably not an impressive vocabulary.

Consider yourself unready for competition until you have developed several strong characters.

For comic IDA, continue to work on developing new characters but now start working on conflict. Remember SOMETHING NEEDS TO HAPPEN in improvised duet acting. Don't just talk about it, DO IT. Incorporate **action** (movement) into your scenes. Sitting and talking becomes very boring for the audience unless you are tremendous comedy writers. Do something that shows action: dance, wrestle, get your coat caught in an elevator door, or climb a ladder. Be creative. Don't copy something you've seen on a television comedy show. Remember your audience may have seen that show too and you are not to copy in this event but to create.

Students can be wonderful scene writers once they get the knack of it. Comedy relies heavily on exaggeration or incongruity so ask yourself how to exaggerate the situation for fun or what would you have to do to make the scene funny because it usually doesn't happen that way. Examples of this could be a bronco rodeo rider taking a ballet lesson or an overweight man in a ladies aerobics class. Practice creating a new scene each day of class. Partners will then get a feel of working together. You will begin to establish a sense of comic timing between you and will have a better feel of playing lines off each other.

Don't get discouraged. Not every scene will work but continue to make sure your scenes have direction and a resolution.

Always practice your conclusion. Know when that scene is to end. Sometimes students just keep talking and talking, going nowhere and it is obvious that they don't know how to end the scene. That is not the final impression you want to leave with the audience. Always practice your conclusion before a performance.

Sometimes you will not be able to create a new character for each round, each tournament. If you did, you might be creating up to twenty-four different characters. So, sometimes you may need to reuse "Sam". Never reuse a character, plot or ending in the same tournament. Always try to be creative and bring something new to each performance. Repetition of this nature is discouraged and sometimes penalized.

At one tournament a judge remarked about a funny IDA he had just seen when another judge indicated he had seen one in a previous round that sounded the same. They discovered it was the same two boys using a plot of a quiz show and the same two characters. No wonder the dialogue seemed so smooth. They were twisting the topic drawn to fit the same plot and characters for each round. Don't set yourself up for disqualification. Your job as an IDA participant is to be original and creative each round.

Another way to be creative in your presentation is to use the provided props as interestingly as possible. The rules in our state indicate the contestants may use a table and two chairs. We have practice sessions utilizing these props in as many ways as possible. For example, turn the table upside down and what could it become in that position? A raft, a flying saucer or a magic carpet. In its upright position, you could get under it as a cave, tunnel or drainpipe. Turn it on its side; now it becomes a barricade, a dressing room for a midget or a boat. Keep thinking of the

multitude of ideas the table could be other than just a table. Do the same with a chair and then with both chairs together and then the chairs with the table. You will be amazed at the number of clever ideas that pop into your mind.

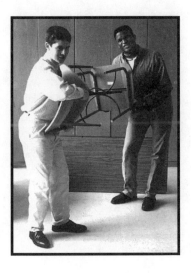

Always check the room where you will be performing **before you draw** your topics. See how sturdy the table and chairs will be and their size. You will then know that you cannot plan an IDA standing on the table if only a card table is provided. It is your obligation to do this checking before you draw. Do not expect them to accommodate your individual performance. You must be ready to use what they provide.

Have fun with your comic IDAs and remember to continually search for innovative ideas.

Some students prefer to do dramatic improvised duet acting scenes. These are often appreciated after watching numerous comic IDAs. If you prefer serious scenes, remember that your characters, plot and resolution must be believable, not forced or exaggerated. Some wonderful dramatic scenes have been created about friendship, betrayal, disagreement or death. Try a serious scene occasionally. You may enjoy it as much as the comic scenes and it certainly gives you a larger range of ideas when selecting a topic. Whichever you choose always remember to include character, plot, conflict (or struggle) and resolution in each scene.

You will be surprised at the variety of topics used in IDA. Be prepared for anything! Sometimes phrases from songs, or unique locations, or exclamations will be the topics drawn. Some example topics are: In the grave yard, life after high school, "Let's Rumba!" or "He went that a way." If a line of dialogue is drawn, sometimes it will be used as the **tag line**, or final line of dialogue in the scene.

Choose your topic quickly. One to two minutes should be sufficient time to make a topic decision. If you have done your homework, most topics will be playable. When you are considering a topic, choose one that allows a possibility of several interpretations or character combinations. Ask friends to give you topics and practice making good decisions, knowing which can be developed and which type lead you to a dead end. Looking at the four previous topic examples, you might be wise to choose the last one and use it as a tag line in your scene. You could create a variety of scenes from "He went that a way." You could create a western scene, a Mafia scene or even perhaps a scene between a tortoise and a hare. Use your imagination. Practice playing several different scenes with different characters using the same tag line.

Don't forget your introduction to your scene. Always include the topic that you drew in your introductory remarks. Be creative. Introduce your scene through your characters, or create a mini-scene to set up information needed in the major scene. Avoid bland opening remarks such as: "We drew *'He Went That-A-Way,'* and our scene takes place on a dude ranch. Mary will play Lariet Lulu and I, John, will play Bronco Billy Bob. We hope you like our scene." Instead you might start with dialogue between the two characters:

Lariet Lulu – Well, howdy Bronco Billy Bob. Where ya been?

Bronco Billy Bob – Oh just over a Laredo. Trying to find out what they did with that no good, thieving cowboy-Roy.

Lariet Lulu – What d'ya find out?

Bronco Billy Bob – Well Lariet Lulu, they let him go. Cain't believe it! When I get my hands on him...

Lariet Lulu – now Billy Bob. Just take it easy. I think I kin help ya out.

Bronco Billy Bob – How's that? What's ya know? Come on, gimme the deetails.

Lariet Lulu – Well now I ain't certain, but I think ....HE WENT THAT A WAY.

Set up that tag line. After a slight pause in line delivery and perhaps in the action, continue the scene and repeat the line as your ending (tag line).

Practice, Practice, Practice! You will have a lot of fun with this event and so will your audience if you do your homework.

TOP NINE TIPS FOR SUCCESS IN IMPROVISED DUET ACTING

1. Know the tournament rules and regulations for improvised duet acting.

2. Choose a partner with whom you can work well.

3. Create possible characters and decide how they might interrelate.

4. Practice scenes daily to establish timing with your partner.

5. Always rehearse your conclusion.

6. Do not copy the work of others.

7. At the tournament, check the props (table and chairs) to use in your performance room before you draw.

8. Continually improve your performance by using your full allotted preparation time.

9. Study your ballots after each contest and make adjustments.

ACTIVITIES

1. Working with a table, create thirty different locations by moving the table into different positions and using your imagination.

2. Create a stance and personal business for these characters:

- a "mad" scientist
- a "hayseed" farmer
- a turtle

- an alien
- an egotistical concert pianist
- a shy five year old

3. Develop a comic scene from these situations:

- tied to the tracks
- fired from work

- winning the lottery
- first day as a beautician

4. Develop a serious scene from these situations:

- death of a friend
- divorce of your parents

- moving your senior year
- winning the lottery

5. Create a scene for each tag line.

- ◦◦ Here today, gone tomorrow.
- ◦◦ It wasn't me!
- ◦◦ Better late than never.
- ◦◦ He was a fighter to the end.

CHAPTER

11

Duo Interpretation

⬤ ⬤

After completing this chapter you should be able to:

❑ Define duo interpretation

❑ Distinguish between duo interpretation and dramatic/ humorous interpretation

❑ Understand the role of physical expression in duo interpretation

❑ Use focal points for character interaction, rather than direct eye contact between characters

⬤ ⬤

New Terms To Learn In This Chapter

Listening

Physical Expression

Visualization

Pose

DUO INTERPRETATION

One of the most exciting new National Forensic League events is duo interpretation. Duo interpretation has been a popular event at the collegiate level and is an event offered in NCFL. Because NFL has added this event, it will become very prominent at invitational tournaments throughout the nation. Some actors are uncomfortable with solo performances. Therefore, duo interpretation offers actors a chance to perform a cutting with a partner. However, duo interpretation is much different from duet acting and therefore is categorized as an interpretation event.

According to the November, 1995 issue of **Rostrum**, the following guidelines apply to duo interpretation.

> Duo interpretations shall not exceed 10 minutes in length. Selections used in duo shall be cuttings from published, printed novels, short stories, plays or poetry. Recorded material that is not printed and published is not acceptable. Adaptations may be for the purpose of continuity only. (If the selection is prose or poetry and contains narration, either or both of the performers may present the narration in addition to the one sustained character.) A cutting must be from a single source. In Duo Interpretation, focus may be direct during the introduction (the performers may look at each other) but must be indirect (offstage) during the performance itself.

Performers may perform multiple characters in duo interpretation. Multiple characters refer to each actor playing more than one character. A sustained character is the portrayal of one character. NFL restricted students to one character the first year, but now allows for each actor to portray multiple characters.

DIFFERENCES BETWEEN DRAMATIC OR HUMOROUS AND DUO INTERPRETATION

Perhaps the chief difference between dramatic interpretation and duo interpretation concerns the use of focal points. In dramatic or humorous, focal points are selected on the basis of the selection. Some monologues have focal points directed toward the audience while most multiple character pieces have focal points directed toward the walls of the room. In other words, the literature dictates the choice of focal points. In duo interpretation focal points are established generally in the back like a multiple character dramatic interpretation. Just like the multiple character dramatic interpretation creates the illusion of two or more characters speaking to each other, so, too, will duo interpretation performers create an illusion of two characters speaking to each other. Unlike duet acting, where actors look at each other as in a stage performance, duo performers may not ever have direct eye contact in the scene, with the exception of the introduction.

Another key difference between duet acting and duo interpretation is the use of movement. There is some discrepancy on the amount of movement allowed in duo interpretation. Many duos remain in interpretation stances, moving the pivot foot and using movement mainly from the waist up. There are others that move far more, resembling a duet scene performed in a drama class. It depends largely on rules established in your state on the movement issue. At the same time there are some exciting blocking possibilities with duo inter-

pretation that enhance the fun of performing and watching this event. On judging duos, NFL has added that duos should be judged on the quality of "**physical expression**." Physical expression would include gesture, pantomime, and movement. In some areas of the country, movement has traditionally been limited. The bottom line on movement is the fact that it should be a necessary outgrowth of the interpretation from the play text.

Another inherent difference concerns the choice of a humorous or dramatic scene. While there is dramatic interpretation and humorous interpretation, duo interpretation is combined and probably will remain so. The choice of literature should be determined , in part, by the preference of the actors. Some performers can handle serious drama, while others are more comfortable with humorous material. You simply have to perform a scene well, be it serious or humorous. If you are more inclined to perform serious literature, you should definitely try it. Again, actors must choose scenes they can handle, if they are to be competitive. In the final round of the first NFL nationals featuring duo interpretation, there were serious and comic scenes. In this competition, a comic scene won first.

Tony Figliola, coach at Holy Ghost Prep, PA, published an article entitled "Duo Techniques" in the February, 1996 issue of **Rostrum**. He has coached high school (NCFL) and college champions in duo interpretation. On the following pages you will find many helpful suggestions from his article.

CUTTINGS

Use one continuous scene, or smoothly and uninterruptedly connect a series of scenes, or link scenes together that logically lead into each other but do not form a continuous whole.

INTRODUCTIONS

Possible methods

1. Each partner alternates the delivery of sentences.

2. One partner adds important words into the sentences spoken by the other.

3. One partner might interrupt/challenge/comment upon the words spoken by the other.

4. One person may be performing a part of the play as the other interweaves the written introduction.

5. One person might sing (or do something physically interesting that is intrinsic to the script and consonant with tone and the character) while the other delivers the intro.

FOCAL POINTS

⊙ When both characters look straight ahead, they are looking at each other.

⊙ When both characters are angled inward, they are looking at each other.

⊙ When both characters turn outward (at perhaps a 45 degree angle) they are addressing each other but not making direct eye contact with each other—perhaps one cooks while the other eats.

⊙ When one character faces front and the other faces sideways, they are not looking at each other—one is obviously attending to something else or may be in another part of the room. The character facing to the side may turn in—face front-to make direct eye contact with the other.

⊙ When one character is out of the scene or picture, s/he usually is turned around; when the entering the scene or the other character's focus, s/he will turn inward 180 degrees.

VISUALIZATION

Although (A) sees (B) while looking straight ahead, (A) should not stare incessantly and unflaggingly at the point/person. As in real human interaction, people avert eye contact-to think, remember, cower, tease, etc.—only to bring it directly back again when a thought is found or courage is mustered, and so on.

LISTENING

On stage, characters, in some way or another, attend to each other. In duo interp, each character must **listen** while the other is speaking. One listens with ears, eyes, face, and body.

PHYSICAL REALIZATION

*"Although many performers in dramatic or humorous interpretation will have one **pose** for each character, it is ill-advised in duo. In Duo, characters must have physical existences justified by the text and kept consistent throughout the performance. But physicality in duo is not a pose; rather, it is a three dimensional body that moves within the initially framed 'body picture,' all the while remaining consistent and true to the psychophysical state justified by character biography. It responds in realistic and 'easy' ways." — Tony Figliola*

The preceding advice by Tony Figliola is useful and important to students and coaches beginning their work in duo interpretation. The entire article in the February, 1996 issue of **Rostrum** provides an excellent framework for your introduction to duo interpretation.

Finally, duo interpretation is an event that presents many creative challenges for future performers. Sharing a forensics event with another person is definitely fun but will have some of the drawbacks like debaters often experience. Occasionally, one person's energy may lag behind the other. Or one actor will make a mistake that will affect the other's performance. Debaters often get impatient with each other when mistakes are made. But good teams realize it is only one round and the only one that counts is the next one. The past is over. So too will duo performers adjust to weaker performances. Such is the nature of any performing. It is equally true of solo performance as well. As much as we try to maintain consistency with our performance, there are rounds that simply don't go as well as others. So work together and be patient with each other as you tackle duo. Cooperation and a positive attitude will bring you far in this exciting event.

REVIEW

TOP NINE TIPS FOR SUCCESS IN DUO INTERP

1. Develop a clear understanding of duo interpretation.

2. Select a scene that fits the capabilities of both actors.

3. If a multiple character scene is chosen, both of you should share in the multiple characterizations. Duo requires equal billing.

4. Establish an introduction that involves both of you.

5. Decide on specific focal points. Adjust focal points depending on the nature of the character interaction.

6. Work on nonverbal reaction to each other's lines.

7. Establish realistic physical attributes for each character.

8. Your timing should fit the piece.

9. Practice, practice, practice.

Appendixes

- **A** ORIGINAL ORATORY TRANSCRIPTS

- **B** EXTEMPORANEOUS TRANSCRIPTS

- **C** EXPOSITORY TRANSCRIPTS

- **D** PLAY PUBLISHING COMPANIES

- **E** APPROPRIATE DRESS

- **F** HOSTING INDIVIDUAL EVENTS TOURNAMENTS

- **G** TOURNAMENT ETIQUETTE

- **H** SAMPLE BALLOTS

Original Oratory Speeches

The following speech was written by Miriam Nalumansi-Lubwama of James Logan High School, California. Miriam's speech earned her a recent California state championship in original oratory and an impressive showing at NFL nationals. She is coached by Tommie Lindsay.

Ever since I was a child, I've always had this fondness for doctors. There was Dr. Stewart, the pediatrician that guided me through a rather accident prone childhood. Dr. Liu, my skilled optometrist, oh and Dr. Michaels, the dentist that wired these contraptions to my teeth to give me that million dollar smile. Of all these doctors, though, there is one who will always be particularly dear to my heart. You see, this man taught me, at the tender age of four, the meaning of life. This man was Dr. Seuss. Of course, I did eventually find out that I couldn't eat green eggs and ham. There was no grinch who stole Christmas, no Mulberry Street existed, and I never did get to see any Cats in a Hat. Most disappointing of all however, was my realization that there are few Hortons in today's world. You see, Horton was an elephant who promised the bird Lazy Mazy that he would sit on her egg for her until she returned. He went through horrible weather, hunters, and innumerable dangers, but through it all he stuck to his promise. In the words of the great Dr. Seuss, Horton the Elephant "Meant what he said, and said what he meant," proving that "an elephants faithful one-hundred percent."

These days, few things can be regarded as one-hundred percent, least of all the idea of the promise. We live in an era when a promise made by no means guarantees a promise kept. The concept of the promise has taken on a whole new meaning. What used to be a person's bond is now little more than a tentative statement of intent, dependant upon one's convenience, or good mood. Now I'll concede that there are times when even the best of intentions can go awry and a promise made in good faith simply can't be kept. But what happens when an entire society stops taking its commitments seriously? Ladies and gentlemen, gone are the Horton's of yesteryear, we are now living in the age of the empty promise.

Responsibility for our commitments is decreasing. It is decreasing on a Societal level, and on a personal level.

Now, we are all familiar with the saying, Nobody's Perfect! Well, I'll be darned if there aren't a million companies out there willing to defy that age old truth and promise us all perfection... that is, for a nominal fee. How many times have you been watching TV or flipping through a magazine only to be seduced by that advertisement asking, "Do you seek the perfect body? Improved intellect, enhanced health, or perhaps all you really need is that... million dollar smile? Well you can have any of the above for just $9.95! Send $10.95 today and you will receive all four. Hey, SATISFACTION GUARANTEED!"-sure sounds like a promise to me. In fact, these are the very miracles Mitchel Friedlander of Fort Lauderdale Florida promised his customers until he was caught and charged with fraud. Even on a larger scale, though, we've been promised everything under the sun. Do you remember the war on drugs, the war on crime, the war on poverty and the revolution in our schools? You should, we've been promised them all. Now certainly none of these promises are bad ideas, or even implausible ones, but at this point our politicians commitments are little more than empty rhetoric, or should I say, empty promises.

My own mother has not made me a promise since I was four years old. Yes, my mother does like me, but she feels that nothing's worse than having to break a promise to a child. You see, most adults, most of the time have the ability to at least question unrealistic promises. Most children aren't quite so lucky. Dr. Haim Ginnott, in his book Between Parent and Child, explains how.

"Promises often build up unrealistic expectations in children." When we promise that favorite toy, or cookie, or anything else to get children to stop crying, a lot of times they take that offering as a serious commitment, and when we don't follow through, Dr. Ginnot continues "the child can come to feel betrayed, or convinced that adults simply can't be trusted."

From our businesses, to our politicians, even ourselves sometimes, the weight of the promise is on the decline. The steadfast elephant seems to be the last strong supporter of commitment to promises. But what about deeper commitments? Are people still keeping their promises where it really matters? Lets take marriage for example. Marriage is perhaps the greatest personal promise individuals make. Indeed Peter and Cornelia Wilson understood the weight of the commitment inherent in wedding vows, which they viewed as promises to God. Their eighty year marriage spanned two World Wars, the Great Depression, and fifteen U.S. Presidents. This couple, though, seems to be of a dying breed. Many people today don't take their spousal promises quite so seriously. Nearly two-thirds of American marriages end in divorce- evidence of phenomenal percentages of broken promises. Most people would agree that parenthood creates some unspoken promise of care and love, yet over seven-hundred parents kill their children each year. Seven-hundred broken promises. Thousands of American teens are impregnated annually, and every time the partner disappears we get yet another broken promise. Love, commitment, and loyalty... easy enough promises to make, but ones we, many times, won't keep.

Just look at the treatment many of our veterans receive. These are men and women who felt so strongly about their commitment to their country, that they were willing to sacrifice everything, but, as one veteran wrote:

God and the military veteran, we adore/In times of danger, not before/The Danger pass'd and all things righted/ God is forgotten, and the veteran slighted.

Forty percent of our male homeless population, and over thirty-five percent of our imprisoned male population are veterans. Not because they are a bad group of people, but more because the promises made to them about adequate job opportunities, health care, and financial support were empty.

What's to blame? Why do people keep making promises they can't keep, or have no intention of keeping? The answer is really quite simple. America has finally, truly, become the land of the free- that is, the guilt free, and the responsibility free. Our word once equivalent to a contractual bond, is now either a comforting gesture, or a bargaining tool. Bill Vitek, professor of philosophy explains "We've become a society of free agents." In our flurry to achieve personal objectives we've adopted a 'me first', a me only, attitude. As emphasis on the self increases, identification with, and commitment in our communities, friends, families and constituencies, is declining. Quite simply, many of us are losing the 'ties that bind'. The more isolated we allow our interests to become from those around us, the easier it is to fudge on commitments made.

As a result of this continual promise making, and promise breaking, many people have become justifiably cynical about those guarantees made to them by friends, professionals, and the government. Sissela Bok, author of the book Lying insists that "The proliferation of frauds has seriously frayed the social fabric... people take for granted that they can't trust." Nowadays, people are going to great lengths to make sure that promises made will hold water. Contracts are drawn up before promises are accepted, as in now common with marriage, or, lawsuits are claimed once a promise has been forfeited. Unlike humans who draw up prenuptial agreements to protect their interests, elephants mate for life—without legal documents to bind them. Ultimately, what we must keep in mind is that the law can only coerce us from the outside, responsibility must govern us inside.

Each of us must decide to accept responsibility for living up to promises made. Furthermore, we all have the power to pressure businesses, the government, and politicians to be accountable for their commitments. Letter-writing, donations to activist groups, and voting against those who fail to keep their promises can all work to foster a climate of social responsibility.

Just imagine what life would be like, if such a climate existed; if each of us viewed promise as Horton did. A myriad of social ills could be avoided by a simple shift in attitude, if we attempted to be more stable and dependable, just like the elephant. Child abuse would cease to be the rampant problem it is today, if people would take seriously their commitment to their children. Politics would no longer be ruled by the mighty dollar, but rather, by politician's commitment to their constituencies. Even "Satisfaction Guaranteed!" could mean something again, if our businesses made an honest effort to live up to their promises. Just imagine what our lives would be like if we committed ourselves to safety, prosperity, and peace... and then stuck to our commitment as Horton did to his.

Then, maybe we too can know that "We meant what we said, and said what we meant" even humans can be faithful "One-hundred percent".

• •

The following speech was written by Natalie Foster of Hutchinson High School, Kansas. Natalie won a recent class 6A state championship in oration with her speech. Natalie is coached by Mr. Richard Young, a member of the NFL hall of fame.

Addicted to crack passed to him in the womb, Matthew left the hospital with Mary Lou Mullins, his foster-mother. Looking into his soft and wisened face, she vowed to love him forever. Months after lovingly nursing the infant back to health, she along with her husband, Scott, confronted the issue of adoption, only to be rebuffed by a social worker. Matthew was black. The Mullins were not. She was told not to even consider it because he was going into a black home no matter how long it took.

Transracial adoption is an issue that has been publicized, debated, and misconstrued. Even if you have no interest in adopting a child, this situation is one that affects us all because it affects the society in which we live. If these children grow up parent-less and we could have prevented it, it falls on each one of us.

This injustice occurs all across the racial spectrum, but I only have 10 minutes. So for the purposes for this speech, we will focus in on one of the most challenged aspects of adoption; placing black children in white homes. We'll see what critics claim is wrong with transracial adoption, the causes, and finally steps we can take to prevent this injustice from spreading.

Since the beginning of our nation there have been glitches within our laws, and I would assert that our philosophy of absolute race matching is one of them. We'll see the absolute need for transracial adoption in our society, the effects of prolonged foster care, and the adverse of race matching.

Current magazine in October, 1994, stated "the percent of minority children in need of homes is far greater than the entire percent of the minority population. For example, in New York, 75% of the 18,000 children up for adoption are black. And social workers are finding it increasingly difficult to place them. Nationwide, that number is 40% contrasted to a 13% population of African-Americans."

If there aren't enough adoptive parents, and clearly there are not, a second problem develops. These excess children are herded into foster care, being shuffled around for possibly their entire lives. In fact, the Washington Post on April 13, 1995, supports me by stating that black children wait "almost twice as long as the national median, and are almost twice as hard to place as children of a different race."

Some people say that if you don't place children with parents of the same race, then they begin to lose their cultural identity. In fact, the National Association of Black Social Workers has long since condemned this practice, labeling it a "cultural genocide." Let me ask you, which the lesser of two evils, placing a child in a home of a different race where he can grow and be nourished in a normal family setting, or in temporary foster care, being moved as often as six months, never gaining a self identity much less a cultural one.

Sometimes these agencies delay placing these children with parents of the wrong race, until efforts are undertaken to find parents of the right race. Does this seem pre-Civil Rights to anyone else? Yet this is the third and final glitch within our laws. Racial matching reinforces racism. In fact, a recent Newsweek article points out that "our philosophy of absolute race matching strengthens the notion that race is destiny, or some sort of dividing line between people, and that love is color, and unless matched, is somehow limited." These ideas are ones that people have given their lives to reverse and will have immeasurable long term effects.

Here is something else for you to consider. Our goal is a colorblind society, correct? How better to teach a child those values than growing up in a mixed race home. How much more tolerant and less concerned will that child be between himself and children of a different color.

By now, you definitely see the plague on our society, the mind set against transracial adoption. I think that you will see the effects aren't written down in black and white and may be unforeseeable. But what causes this problem? I contend it is two separate roots, our leaders and our misguided law.

Minority leaders have played a monumental roll in shaping civil rights to what it is today. Due to the NABSW, condemnation of transracial adoption and the effect it generated, many black children since then have been left in a lurch because today's social workers don't want to step across this politically charged area, and therefore played the traditional roll of race matching. In fact, black leaders and prominent figures have consistently backed the social workers on the notion that transracial adoption equals a cultural genocide. Now this long heralded idea has been proven absolutely false.

Alstein and Simon, two professors at American University, undertook the longest and most conclusive study done on the subject. They worked with 204 racially UN-matched families, and their findings were the exact opposite. They found these families, and especially the children were confident, secure, and not racially confused. In fact, they responded to researchers questions on race with oblivion we see demonstrated through society, and ultimately, our adoptive system, and were comfortable with themselves and who they were as a person.

While a lot of the blame rests upon our attitudes, some it can be attributed to our laws. The most recent breakthrough on the subject was a bill passed in Congress, tacked inconspicuously to the bottom of the GOP's welfare portion of the Contract with America. This bill as stated in Current magazine says, "We are going to place black children with black parents, but if you can't then go ahead and place them with while." While this has good intentions I am not sure what this is changing nor solving. It is still placing a preference on race not competency and is leaving perfectly capable adoptive families on a waiting list for a long period of time while social workers wait for parents of the same race to magically appear.

This bill goes on to state that an agency may consider a child's cultural, ethnic and racial backgrounds to be placed, but only on an individualized basis. The problem with this is that it leaves too much to the ideas of the social worker, and allows leeway for those that oppose transracial adoption hundreds of reasons to prevent it.

Finally, a third barrier arises. Forty-three states within our union bar transracial adoption, even unofficially or though actual laws. You now see that the problem is at the very core of our society. While those that oppose what is happening, then actions are not futile, and there is still much more that can be done and I hope that you will adopt my philosophies.

First, we must fix our laws. Then each American, must change their outlook. Members of Congress who wrote this bill, while flawed, provides and important first step in awareness. But the battle is far from over. We cannot be content with the way things currently stand. We must push for a tougher guideline and a more explicit stance on this practice which contradicts all that we believe in. In fact, I think we need legislation outlining a time period, minimal, if any, that a social worker is allowed to wait before placing a child with parents of a different race. I also think we need to change our adoptive systems philosophy to one of competency and what is best for the child.

However, legislation alone cannot solve our problems. We must focus our attitudes to reinforce its acceptance. Remember, 40% of orphans will not be adopted unless we as Americans tear down our barriers to transracial adoption. The fact lies within our own perceptions.

For example, if you hear of someone talking derogatorily about a family of mixed race, clue them in on reality. Tell them of the black children waiting to be adopted, tell them of the situation we are currently in... Tell them of little Matthew and the Mullins. Because if you don't, who will?

Finally, if you have adopted a child of a different race, Dr. Towell a psychologist in Chicago urges you to tell your child early on of the racism they are about to encounter. Prepare them for the ugly place that growing up can often be to anyone different. It will better prepare them for life.

You know, I'd like to be able to stand before you today and tell you that little Matthew got go home with the Mullins and grow up a normal, happy life. But unfortunately, due to our laws, our leaders, and our lack of acceptance... he did not.

Extemporaneous
Speaking Speeches

United States Extemporaneous Speaking

• •

The following speech was delivered by Doug Miller of Concordia High School, Kansas, in the final round of United States extemporaneous speaking at a recent National Forensic League national tournament. Doug, a four time national qualifier in US extemporaneous speaking, is coached by Mr. Glenn Nelson.

Don Herold once said that "poverty must have many satisfactions, else there wouldn't be nearly as many poor people." However, if you were to ask one of the millions of Americans who lives at, or below, the poverty level, they would tell you that Mr. Herold is simply off his rocker, for obviously poverty has few, if any satisfactions at all. Thus, it is in examining how the United States can put an end to the plight of many of its underprivileged citizens, I believe it important to ask the question, "Should all Americans be guaranteed a minimum standard of living?"

Now, the answer to this question is a definite "yes they should, as long as they try and help themselves." We find this for three compelling reasons. First, because they've paid for it and deserve it. Second, because the problem of poverty affects all American citizens, and third, because there are, unfortunately, a large number of freeloaders, for example, in our welfare system.

When examining the first major reason why all Americans should be guaranteed a minimum standard of living, at least as long as they try and help themselves, is because they've paid for it , and deserve it. Now the world-renown physicist Albert Einstein once stated "The hardest thing in the world to understand, is the income tax." If a man of Albert Einstein's intellect couldn't understand it, then it is highly unlikely that the rest of America has any chance to do so. But even though we don't fully understand it, we continue, year in and year out, to pay it. Examining why this is so, the February 3 edition of the Economist magazine states, because the constitution gives the government the authority to do so. Unfortunately, while many Americans feel that their money is just going into a giant black hole and will never be seen again it seems that just the opposite it true, for as the April 15 edition of U.S. News and World Report points out that the money collected as income tax goes first and foremost toward trying to improve this nation, but secondly toward creating an insurance policy for American citizens. If they fall of the bandwagon, the government will be there to help them bounce back. And this is why the April 4 edition of the Christian Science Monitor points out that the US should guarantee a minimum standard of living for all of its citizens because they've paid their dues in terms of their income tax, and thus the federal government should return the trust that has been placed in it by ensuring that if its citizens do fall on hard times, the federal government will be there to take care of them.

But we see that while it is obvious that creating a minimum standard of living will benefit American's poorer individuals, it will also benefit the rest of America as well. Thus leading us to the second major reason as to why all Americans should be guaranteed a minimum standard of living, at least as long as they try and help themselves. That being because the problem of poverty affects all American citizens. And as Jasmine point out earlier in this round (referring to another speech by an earlier competitor) it is true that "no man is an island." And as the May 4 edition of the Washington Post points out, that is no more there than here, in this nation, where often you can hardly ever get away from your fellow countrymen. And that is why it is important for the United States to truly address the problem of poverty, for we find that affects all American citizens. As the New York Times states in its April 28 edition, if someone is unemployed, they have less money to spend, thus bringing consumer spending down, and thereby bringing the economy down with it. Also, if someone doesn't have adequate health insurance, they go to the emergency room for treatment and often times can't pay for it, thus putting those high prices back upon the health insurance premiums on the rest of America's citizens. This has prompted Business Week magazine to state in its April 1 edition that it is vital for America to maintain a minimum standard of living for all of its citizens for due to the fact that first, it is obviously beneficial for those Americans who live at, or below, the poverty level, but more importantly to the rest of us, it affects all American citizens in their own pocket books. Thus if the US can maintain a minimum standard of living for all of its citizens, then the entire nation can save a little bit of cash.

But while it is obvious that the US should try and implement a minimum standard of living for all of its citizens, unfortunately, we must attach a few strings to it. That being because of the third major reason why all Americans should be guaranteed a minimum standard of living, at least as long as they try and help themselves, that being because there are , unfortunately, many freeloaders, for example, in our welfare system.

It is obvious that the issue of welfare has been one of the most hotly contested issues in this nation over the last few years. As it is pointed in the April 10 edition of the Kansas City Star, one of the major reasons for this is because many Americans try to abuse the system, for a recent Department of Health and Human Service study points out, of those Americans who are currently on welfare, more than 40% have been on welfare for the last five years. Thus this has prompted the April 8 edition of Newsweek magazine to point out that many Americans are trying to use the welfare system to their own advantage and thus not give back to the nation that has given so much to them. And that is why the May 15 edition of the Christian Science Monitor states that the US, while it should provide a minimum standard of living for all of its citizens, must attach a few conditions, those being that the American citizens who are receiving assistance should at least try and help themselves. For example, they should go out and try and achieve their high school equivalency degree, or acquire job training so they can be come more employable. Thus, the US, by lending a helping hand to those citizens who deserve it, can make this nation a better place for all of it citizens.

So when reflecting back upon the question, "Should all American citizens be guaranteed a minimum standard of living?" We see that the answer is a definite "yes they should, just as long as they try and help themselves," due to the fact that first, we've paid into the system and deserve it, second, the problem of poverty affects all American citizens, and third, because unfortunately, there are still a large number of freeloaders, for example, in our welfare system.

So while Don Herold may have been incorrect in this statement, that poverty has hardly any real satisfactions, it appears that the United States, in order to stop this problem, should implement a minimum standard of living for all of its citizens, so no one in this country has to go through dire economic conditions.

Foreign Extemporaneous Speaking

The following speech was presented by Ben Lerner of Topeka High School, Kansas in the final round of foreign extemporaneous speaking at a recent National Forensic League national tournament. Ben is coached by Pam McComas.

The famed American wittest P.J. O'Rourke once contended "We've never been a good neighbor to Mexico. After all, we stole half their country and it was the half with paved roads." O'Rourke's rather humorous sentiment has a specific political application to the current state of North American affairs. As the stability of Mexico is unquestionably inter-linked with our prosperity and stability in the north. From the perspective of a nation with a vested interest in the peaceful evolution of the framework of Mexican democracy and eventual prosperity, it's essential to evaluate whether or not Mexico poses significant threats to the international order we hold so dear, and to specifically pose the question, "Will Mexico present the next big crisis in foreign affairs?" Hearteningly, the answer to this question is a definitive no.

The substantiation for my optimism comes through the consideration of three separate areas of analysis. Initially one must consider how the Mexican economy is stabilizing. Second of all, we must examine how political democracy is solidifying. And third and finally, we must conclude with the analysis that domestic politics in Mexico are finally settling down.

The first reality of the current situation in Mexico is that the economy that was so rocked by financial instability has finally stabilized. The June 16 edition of The Washington Post National Weekly contended that after contracting by an overwhelming 7% of the Mexico economy has consistently expanded by 3 and 4% respectively in the last 2 quarters. A recent edition of the Paris based daily La' Monde solidified this perspective when it contended that many in the international community doubted the ability of the Mexican economy to be flexible but recent activities not only on the level of privatizing, but of economic expansions as a whole have proved those skeptics wrong. A January edition of the Christian Science Monitor concurs when it contends that the Mexican economy has proven itself able to react to its own deficiencies . This reasoning leads up to the heartening conclusion that Mexico's economic stability is a constant to our south.

Now although the Mexican economy might not easily ever regain the predominance it once enjoyed, it is clear that economic stability is not going to be threatened by the domestic political concerns of Mexico. From the perspective of the United States and the rest of the globe that were rocked by the domestic financial crisis two years ago, it's important to remember that the economic stability of Mexico is an economic stabilizing constant in North America as a whole.

But as the famous anarchist Emma Goldman once contended, politics is the reflex of the economic sphere, and having established the economic nature of the current situation in Mexico, it is now essential to look to our second political reason why a foreign affairs crisis is not imminent and that is that political democracy is being solidified within the nation of Mexico. A recent addition of Foreign Policy Magazine contended that democracy is a prerequisite to meaningful stability to our south. The policies analysis was essentially this. As long as Mexico can not provide a democratic framework, it can never have the domestic political stability or the economic liberalization necessary to be prosperous. A recent edition of the Mexico City's daily La Hornada solidified this perspective when it contended that democratic reform in Mexico has to first be meaningful in order for economic liberalization to ever bear fruit. The February 28th edition of the British based Economist Magazine contends that Ernesto Zedeo Ponce de Leon, the president of Mexico has taken significant strides to solidifying the current economic and politically democratic system in Mexico. It points to two specific actions as being important. The first was the conclusion of a monopoly that the revolutionary institutional party or PRI currently holds on television in the electoral system. And secondly, it ended an equally important monopoly on the colors of the national flag. A psychologically important issue considering that only the PRI the party that's been in power for 65 years ever had the opportunity to expose the colors of the nation. Which in the words of a June 17th edition of the Nation magazine created a psychological residue of elections that the PRI and the state were inseparable. But as Mexican presidential candidate, Luis Donaldo Colosio once contended, "the winds of change are sweeping across Mexico." After having established two of the important current situations, it is essential to now consider that the political destabilizing gayo that Calosio once discussed is settling into stable domestic and democratic winds. For the domestic politics of Mexico are finally settling down. A recent edition of El Tiempo , a Honduras based periodical, contended that within Mexico City people such as Marcos, the leader of the Zaptista Liberation Army, whose responsible for the violent insurgency in the southern break-away state of Giapas are glamorized across the nation. Specifically, the journal contended that he is considered not only to represent the dissatisfaction of the South, but also to represent the nation's dissatisfaction with the government domestically as a whole. However, a recent edition of the Guardian of London newspaper contended that consistently although Mexicans are unsatisfied with their political system, domestic stability is returning largely because people no longer identify the failures with the current President Ernesto Zedeo Ponce de Leon. But rather, his seemingly corrupt predecessor, Carlos Selenas. This realization is leading many to conclude that domestic politics within the state of Mexico are finally settling down.

And from the perspective of a nation that know the potential destabilizing effects of non-tranquil Mexico politics, it is essential to remember that if the economy is stable, if democracy can be maintained, and if domestic politics will remain calm, we have nothing to fear from our neighbor to the south. It then seems that the words from a recent journal of Foreign Affairs, were not only emphatic, but accurate. That in conclusion, the Mexican American relationship will not only be the greatest opportunity for prosperity into the next century, but one of the closest political closely knit relationships in the history of the world.

With that in mind and reexamining the question, "Will Mexico present the next big crisis to foreign affairs?", we arrive at the heartening answer that it will most definitely will not. For the economic stability that was so long fought for to our south, coupled with the ability of the government to begin meaningful political, democratic reforms and third and finally, the settling down of the Mexican's domestic political system has created an environment where we can prove P.J. O'Rourke's humorous, but cynical statement incorrect and finally pursue policies of joint prosperity that would allow for us and Mexico to have a prosperous relationship into the future.

Expository Speaking Speeches

•••

The following expository speech was written by Jennifer Liu of Leland High School, California. Jennifer's speech recently earned her the title of California state champion in expository speaking. She is coached by Gay Brasher.

"WHAT'S IN A NAME?"

Hello? Oh hi! Is this Jim? Yeah, I'm Mary's cousin. Yeah, I'm a little nervous about our blind date too. My name? It's Hildegard. Hello? Hello?!

Okay, what just happened here? Well, after hearing that he'd be going out with... Hildegard, Jim probably decided that maybe he didn't want to go on that blind date after all. But wait, just because of a name? Whether Jim and Hildegard realized it or not , our names play a much bigger role in our lives than most of us realize. They affect how people see us, who we become, and in Hildegard's case, our ability to attract the opposite sex. Names. We all have them, and we even know other people who do too, but most of us still don't take the time to stop and ask ourselves: "What's in a name?"

"What's in a name? A rose by any other name would smell as sweet." Or would it? Even Juliet herself didn't believe it, and many recent studies suggest that you shouldn't either. In a study at Tulane University, people were shown pictures of equally attractive women. But when the pictures were labeled with the names Kathy, Jennifer, and Christine, four out of five people said that they were more attractive than pictures labeled Ethel, Harriet, and Gertrude. In another study at U.C. San Diego, a group of elementary school teachers were all given the same papers to grade. And get this: the researchers found that the teachers gave higher grades to the papers labeled with more popular names. Karen and Lisa out-scored Bertha by a few points, and Michael and David out-scored Elmer and Hubert by a full letter grade. But wait, don't start naming your daughters Jennifer and Christine just yet, especially if you want them to get a good job. A study conducted at Rensselaer Polytechnic revealed a prejudice in corporate hiring against women with attractive names. Names like Heather and Adrienne were considered too sexy to be executive material, while Mildred and Cornelia seemed destined for corporate success. Sorry Christine, but Cornelia got the job.

But names don't just affect the impressions we make, they also influence the people we become. British psychologist Helen Petrie found that girls with exceedingly feminine names did in fact have more girlish personalities. Studies also show that young women with uncommon names are more likely to be emotionally secure. Guys, on the other hand, don't fare as well. In a group of criminal men with similar backgrounds who had committed similar crimes, the men with unusual names had perpetrated four times as many crimes as those with common ones.

But if you live in Germany, you don't have to worry about any of this. In Germany, any name that might endanger the well-being of the child is forbidden by law.

But in the United States, parents can name their children anything they want. Unfortunately, some parents take this freedom a little too far. Real children have actually been given names like Pitbull, Shackles, and even Nausea. A well-known family in Texas named their daughter Ima. What's wrong with that? Well, her last name was Hogg. Along with poor Ima Hogg, other children have been named Seymour Hare, Ben Dover, Mary Rhoda Duck, and ...Eureka Garlic.

But luckily, most parents in America choose to be trendy rather than cruel. So let's take a look at exactly what these trends have been. Today the most popular names for newborns are Jessica and Michael. The most popular names for people my age are Jennifer, and Michael again. For adults the most common names are Mary, Linda, Robert, and Michael, yet again. It seems as if you can find a Michael just about anywhere; in fact, about one out of every thirty males is named Michael - it's been the most popular name for nearly half a century. But Michael is just a passing fad when compared to Mary and John. Until the 1900's, Mary and John had been the most popular names for three centuries. In 1830, nearly one out of every six girls was named Mary, and in the middle ages, one-fourth of all English boys were named John.

Yet maybe these times of less originality were easier to live in. If everyone were named Mary and John, none of us would ever have to worry about forgetting people's names. Yet forgetting names is an age-old problem. In ancient Rome, politicians actually hired servants to walk ahead of them to remind them of the names of people who were approaching. Today, remembering names is just as important. Like Dale Carnegie said in his bestselling book How To Win Friends And Influence People, "There is no sound sweeter than a person's own name." Studies show that when you use someone's name in a conversation, they're a hundred and fifty percent more aware that you're there. On the flip side, forgetting people's names can be damaging to your business and personal relations. In fact, the fear of forgetting people's names create so much stress that many people choose to avoid social events altogether. Estimates say that at social events, as much as 95% of a person's brain power is funneled into trying to remember people's names.

Yet for a few of us, the sound of our own name may not be so sweet. In a survey of young adults, one out of every six of them wished he or she had a different name, and hundreds of these people do change their names every day. So how do you change your name: Depending on what county you live, it usually takes about one or two trips down to the courthouse, a few weeks, and about two hundred dollars. It may sound a bit pricey, but for a whole new identity, two hundred dollars is a bargain investment. Ralph Slovenko, a professor of psychiatry, says that, "...for many people, a name change can be better than plastic surgery. It's a form of therapy for those who literally want to become someone else."

Consider Hollywood, where a name can make... or break your career. Now, we all know how Norma Jean Baker changed her name to Marilyn Monroe, but did you know that Judy Garland's real name was Francis Gumm? And that John Wayne, the all-American hero, was really named Marion, Marion Morrisson. And what about Whoopi Goldberg? That's right, Whoopi Goldberg is not Whoopi Goldberg's real name. Her real name was Caryn Johnson. Not quite as exciting, is it?

But while name changes can mean fame and success for aspiring actors and actresses, for others, they often mean pain and sacrifice. Throughout history, many Jews changed their identities to escape religious persecution, and a name change was often an inevitable sacrifice. More recently, Bosnian Muslims have been taking on Serbian names to escape ethnic cleansing by the Serbs. Yet many of them refused to change their names - because it would mean sacrificing their culture and identity. But as result, Serbian military groups have driven them out of their homes, robbed them, and then herded them out of the city, causing them to lose everything they have worked their whole lives for, their homes and businesses, their families, their freedom, and sometimes, even their lives.

Who would have thought that something as simple and common as a name could play such a powerful and extraordinary role in our lives? Take a look at your own name. Not only does it affect how people see you, but it more than likely has shaped who you are today. And although many of us take them for granted, our names are one of our most cherished possessions. Perhaps this explains what they say in the Cheers theme song: "You wanna' go where everybody knows your name." What's in a name? A lot.

● ●

The following expository speech was written by Sarah R. Bahr of Caney Valley High School, Kansas. Sarah presented her speech in the final round of expository speaking at a recent NFL national tournament. Sarah is coached by Kathy Falkenberry.

"JUST LEFT OF RIGHT"

At the turn of the century, a primitive tribe was discovered in a remote area of South America. Cultural similarities were found between this tribe and some Native American tribes, yet one bizarre custom distinguished these people from all others. It seems that soon after the birth of a child, tribesmen spent some time observing the motor skills of the infant. If the child demonstrated any tendency toward left handedness, he or she was immediately destroyed.

This action was taken because the clansmen felt that a left-handed person was the personification of evil and would ultimately bring about the demise of the tribe.

This terrible incident is an extreme example of discrimination against left-handers and it gives amazing insight on the treatment of lefties throughout the years.

Now many of you may think that because I am giving this speech that I am left handed, but, I'm not. My older sister Amber is however and I must admit that there are times today when I wish this ancient tribes custom were still in effect today. Just kidding. But, an estimated 13% of the world's population is found to be left-handed, which may be a blessing to those who prefer to be a "breed apart". The right side of the brain (the artistic, fun side of the brain) dominates in left-handers. This is substantiated by the fact that several great composers, artists, and entertainers are southpaws.

Michaelangelo and Raphael, along with Picasso and Dá Vinci were all lefties. Bach composed left handed and Hendrix jammed with his left hand. Leaders such as Caesar, Napoleon, Franklin, Roosevelt, Bush and Clinton all used their left hand as the dominate hand of use. Tom Cruise is left handed. So is Oprah. Julia Roberts used her left hand to dip strawberries into champagne in her film PRETTY WOMAN.

Creativity isn't the only good point of being left-handed. There are other advantages as well. On toll roads, lefties have advantage when throwing exact change into the bucket. Left-handed boxers throw opponents off balance in the right.

Left-handed batters have a 2 step head start running to 1st base and a curve ball is less intimidating when it come from the outside part of the plate. Look no further than the hall of fame for proof: one half of all honored hitters are left handed.

That is the GOOD NEWS for left-handers. The BAD NEWS, as expressed in the opinion of Dr. Stanley Coren, a psychologist at the University of British Columbia in Vancouver is that left-handers may have a 9 year shorter life span than that of right-handers. Coren's study shows that left handers should be on the endangered species list.

The study concludes that lefties are 85% more likely to be injured in automobile accidents, 55% more likely to hurt themselves with tools, and 6 times as likely to die of accident related injuries than right-handers. Others conclude that southpaws exhibit higher incidences of suicide, homosexuality, insomnia, schizophrenia, retardation, and asthma.

Contrary to this stereotype, lefties aren't any more maladroit than the rest of us. It's just the rest of the world is exclusively designed with the right-hander in mind.

But, for those of you that are left handed, don't worry because several organizations for lefties have been formed to help lefties overcome some of the barriers that are put up against them in society. One of the most prominent voices for lefties in the world is Left-handers International stationed in Topeka, Kansas. It specialized in left-handed mail order items that lefties need to get along with this cold, cruel, right handed world. They have also established a legal counsel service for cases of discrimination aimed at left handers.

They have been celebrating International Left-handers' Day on August 13 since 1976 and will hold their 20th birthday this upcoming August. They honor many prominent southpaws for their accomplishments and special uniqueness of being a famous leftie.

One recent honorees was General Norman Schwarzkopf. The retired general swings a good club and baseball bat right handed. But everything else including fighting wars he does left handed. In his front office in Washington, the General had this aphorism hung on the wall.

"Everyone is born left handed. They only become right handed after they commit their first sin."

Thankfully, the custom of the ancient tribe of killing each left-handed child did not carry over to our culture, for if it did, we would be without some of the most influential men and women of our time and I would be an only child.

Play Publishing Companies

Play Publishing Companies which have play list catalogues.

Baker's Plays
100 Chauncy Street
Boston, MA 02111
617-482-1280

Dramatic Publishing Co.
311 Washington St. P.O. Box 129
Woodstock, Illinois 60098
815-338-7170

Dramatists Play Service
440 Park Avenue South
New York, N. Y. 10016
212-683-8960

Samuel French, Inc.
45 West 25th St.
New York, N.Y. 10010-2751
212-206-8990

Musical Publishing Companies which have catalogues.

Music Theatre International
545 Eighth Avenue
New York, N.Y. 10022
212-868-6668

Rodgers and Hammerstein Library
598 Madison Avenue
New York, N.Y. 10018
212-486-0643

Samuel French, Inc. Musical Dept.
45 West 25th St.
New York, N.Y. 10010
212-206-8125

Tams-Witmark Music Library, Inc.
560 Lexinton Avenue
New York, N. Y. 10022
212-688-2525

Other sources you may wish to contact:

Applause Books
211 West 71st Street
New York, N.Y. 10023
215-595-4735

Edna Means Dramatic Service
610 Harmon Street
Tama, Iowa 52339
515-484-3440

Pioneer Drama Service
P.O. Box 4267
Englewood, CO. 80155-4267
303-779-4035

Tournament Dress

Think about what you will wear to the tournament and the image you will convey to your judge. Judges don't know you at all. What image will they receive? Will it be that of a responsible, intelligent, talented student or will they see someone who looks like they came in from washing the car. Take pride in forensics and represent the event well. You may think that what you wear should not matter and it probably shouldn't but it does. You don't need expensive clothes but you need clean and appropriate clothing. Remember that each tournament is special; it's not an aerobics class so sweats and tennis shoes are not appropriate.

Female competitors need to be particularly careful about the length of their skirt or dress. When skirt lengths go up, duet acting and improvised duet acting movements are limited tremendously. Consider opting for a longer dress. Before you leave for a tournament, always sit before a floor length mirror to check the appropriateness of a skirt or dress length. Keep evening wear for evening. That includes low- cut tops, see through blouses and extremely high heels.

Everyone needs to practice good personal hygiene before a tournament. This includes clean body, hair, and teeth. Females must also be careful with makeup. Don't overdo it. Sometimes overdone eye makeup appears comical. Make sure your hair is groomed and off your face, especially off the eyebrows for interpretative reasons. Overbearing or noisy jewelry should be left at home.

Dressing conservatively is safer for competition's sake.

Hosting An Invitational Events Tournament

PLANNING STAGES

Have a squad meeting to discuss the details of the tournament. First set the date. Try to obtain a list of dates of other invitationals in your state. Check with other area schools for such a list or contact your state activities association. After selecting a date check with activities director at school to make sure there are no conflicts with the use of the building.

Write a letter of invitation including all pertinent details of the tournament. Explain the events offered in the tournament and the number of total entries allowed. Provide information for lodging, a time schedule of rounds, rules and procedures of the tournament, entry deadlines, awards, the number of schools or entries you will accept, and any other necessary information. The letter should reflect a cordial tone. Make your invited schools truly want to come to your tournament. Several squad members can participate in the addressing and stuffing of invitations.

With your coach's assistance, order medals and sweepstakes trophies. Your coach will advise you on the availability of funding. Entry fees paid by the school should offset such expenditures.

Establish committees and chairpersons for each committee. Committees should include the following:

TOURNAMENT DIRECTOR

A student director should be chosen to oversee the details of the tournament. Your coach may assist with the necessary preparation. Some squads allow the president of the speech team to direct the tournament. It is generally one of the older members of the team. The squad must trust that the individual can accept and fulfill the responsibilities of the position.

JUDGES

Several students should be responsible for calling previous judges for your tournament. The judge's chair should also get each member of the squad to find five or ten rounds of judging, depending on the anticipated size of the tournament. Start early on this task. It is perhaps the most time consuming and challenging aspects of hosting a tournament.

If you rely on many community judges with little previous experience, a judges clinic is often helpful. Members of the squad can demonstrate the events and your coach can explain the nature of each individual event. A video tape can also be shown for demonstration purposes.

TAB ROOM

Tab room personnel should consist of responsible students. Students must be careful and accurate when tab room responsibilities are performed. When scores are recorded, one should read and the other should record the ranks and quality points. Scores should be written in pencil the first time. To double check accuracy the students should reverse the roles and the scores may be recorded in pen. Never allow only one person to read and record scores. It is very easy to make a mistake.

Tabulation sheets should be prepared in advance with space for codes, names, rank, rate, and sweepstakes points. Packets should be made for each school for ballots. It is wise to put two students in charge of stuffing the ballots. All competitors want to see their ballots after the tournament.

The tournament director, with the help of tab room personnel, can schedule the tournament. Your coach may choose to do the scheduling. When scheduling, balance the number competing in each section. Depending on the size of the tournament, five to seven in each section is preferable. Try to variate the competition in each round. Avoid placing members of the same school in the same section, unless they have more entries than the number of sections. If speaking order is followed, variate it for each contestant. After a scheduled is typed, double check it for errors. Make sure all contestants are competing in every round. Save copies of schedules from reputable tournaments. They can be a good reference for students scheduling for the first time.

RUNNERS

Have one student serve as the chair of runners. This person should check off ballots as they come in, making sure that ballots are received from all rooms. If the squad is large enough, assign runners to three or four rooms. The runner can personally collect the ballots from the judges, checking to see that ranks and rates are given. Catching mistakes when the judge is present is preferable. Runners can save tab room personnel many problems by detecting mistakes and getting them corrected. Runners are optional, but helpful if you have the personnel.

TIMEKEEPERS

Appoint a chair for timekeepers. Timekeepers should be used for draw events such as extemporaneous or impromptu. If your squad can recruit enough timers for all events, that is preferable. However, judges often time contestants. Timekeepers are helpful, but not required.

EXTEMPORANEOUS PREP ROOM

Extemp questions can be written by extempers on the squad. Your coach should read all questions before the tournament, checking the wording of the questions and the fairness of the questions. Appoint at least two students to monitor the extemp draw and prep room. Efforts must be made to keep the extemp room quiet, so contestants can do their best work preparing for speech. The tournament director should also monitor the extemp room to make sure things are going well.

HOSPITALITY ROOM

The hospitality room is a place for judges and coaches to relax. Food and drinks should be provided for them. Unless you have a budget, members of the squad can provide the food and drink for the lounge. Have each member volunteer to bring a food item or drink. Also, appoint a chair and two helpers. Students can call local businesses and seek donated food. Businesses are often glad to help the local schools. Make sure you write a thank you letter. It is important to thank each business in your school packet. A well supplied hospitality room will improve your personal relations with the community judges and the coaches in attendance.

REGISTRATION

A packet should be prepared prior to the day of the tournament. It should consist of:

- ❏ Ballots
- ❏ Schedules
- ❏ Maps
- ❏ Rules and regulations
- ❏ Judging assignments for the sponsor or coach
- ❏ A sweeps sheet for names and code numbers

At registration the tournament director should make a list of all cancellations. If possible try to accommodate schools wanting extras to fill out for the cancelled entries. Checks will need to be receipted in a school receipt book. Have a school list with the amount owed. Make sure you give the checks to your coach after registration.

A FINAL CAUTION

There will be problems in any tournament. Your squad must have patience. A tournament always sees worse from the inside than it really is on the outside to the competitors. Students should try not to get noticeably upset about problems. Problems can be solved more effectively with a calm approach than an angry one. There are problems that are beyond the control of host school. Deal with them as they come up in a positive manner. Be patience and proud that you are providing the opportunity for your fellow schools to receive the benefits of speech education.

Tournament Etiquette Guidelines

As a member of a forensic squad you are a representative of your school; thus, your actions and behavior are part of your school's reflection. It is important that you remember at all times that you are an extension of your school and coach. Don't give your school a bad forensics reputation because you don't know proper tournament etiquette.

1. Enter your host school with a positive attitude about your competition.

2. Keep hallway noise minimal. Judges and performers dislike distracting hallway noise. A judge could feel sorry for the contestant performing and angry at you for creating the disturbance. Close the door when you are performing and leave the door open when you have completed your performance and the judge is waiting for the next contestant.

3. Never use foul language at a tournament.

4. Horseplay, toys and practical jokes are distractions and do not belong at a tournament. You are there for competition. Watch others perform or support your own team by being present for their performances.

5. Realize that some school districts do not have the same outstanding facilities as you do. Be grateful that they host a tournament and you were invited.

6. Avoid speaking negatively about your judge. Future judges could hear this and it could prejudice them in a close round. In addition, it is often difficult to obtain judges, and many parents and friends have volunteered their time.

7. Graciously learn to live with the conditions and tournament rules whether it be walking outside in rainy weather, performing in a locker room or adjusting to a new category of competition.

8. Never smoke, drink alcohol or take illegal drugs at a tournament.

9. Respect the property of the host school. Vandalism or theft at another school or to another team is reason for immediate dismissal from your squad.

10. At the awards assembly, sit with your squad. Do not put your legs over the backs of the chairs. Remove hats in the building.

11. Applaud both your team's success and the success of your competition.

12. Avoid grandstanding your own personal success. In other words, practice some humility.

13. Read your ballots on the bus or van after you have left the host school. It is difficult to contain your feelings about judges and the host school when you feel you did not receive the ratings you deserved.

By following these few guidelines you will be representing your school well and saving your coach many embarrassing situations.

APPENDIX
H

Sample Ballots

On the following pages you will
find sample ballots for the following events:

- Original Oration
- Oral Interpretation (Prose)
- Oral Interpretation (Poetry)
- Solo Acting (Serious)
- Solo Acting (Humorous)
- Duet Acting
- Improvised Duet Acting
- Extemporaneous Speech
- Informative Speech
- Impromptu Speaking

KANSAS STATE HIGH SCHOOL ACTIVITIES ASSOCIATION
SPEECH & DRAMA INVITATIONALS, FESTIVALS & CHAMPIONSHIPS
ORIGINAL ORATION

"An original oration shall be defined as a memorized, original, persuasive speech with a unique approach to a universal theme, demonstrating outstanding qualities of logic, organization, language and delivery, and rising above the commonplace in its impact." — *KSHSAA Speech and Drama Manual*

NAME and/or CODE # _____   SCHOOL and/or CODE # _____

TITLE _____   ROUND _____   ROOM _____

Judge's Signature _____

Please write judge's comments on the back of this ballot.
Remember, this is to be a learning experience.

Organization and Thought Content

A. Is the subject matter intrinsically worthwhile?

B. Is the approach fresh, original in its concept and free from the more stereotyped cliches?

C. Are the contents of the speech arranged in the most effective manner?

Voice and Diction

A. Is the language of the speech appropriate, communicative and forceful?

B. Is the voice pleasant, distinct and responsive?

Delivery

A. Is the speaker sincere, direct, animated and persuasive?

B. Is there an absence of distracting gestures, quirks and mannerisms?

C. Is the speech itself delivered in the best accepted manner of oratory?

Time Limit: Entrants exceeding the ten-minute time limit shall be penalized as indicated on the reverse side. Students may complete last sentence. *(Please indicate if excessive time applies.)* There is no minimum time requirement.

Participant's Information: Please remember that the sections of your ballot do not carry equal weight. Each judge is allowed to determine the percentage evaluation of each section.

KSHSAA SPEECH & DRAMA
INVITATIONALS—FESTIVALS—CHAMPIONSHIPS

RANK CONTESTANTS CONSECUTIVELY (1st = BEST)
Circle **ONE RANK ONLY.** *No two contestants may receive the same rank.*

1st   2nd   3rd   4th   5th   6th   7th   8th   9th   10th

Circle **ONE NUMBER ONLY** (25 = BEST) for **QUALITY POINTS** or **TOURNAMENT RATING**
Contestants may receive the same quality points or tournament rating.

25 24 23 22 21   20 19 18 17 16   15 14 13 12 11   10 9 8 7 6

SPEECH & DRAMA FESTIVALS
Circle **ONE ROMAN NUMERAL** (I = BEST) for **DIVISION RATING**

I   II   III   IV

NOTE: These are available from the KSHSAA. See order blank in *KSHSAA Speech and Drama Manual*

(OVER)   Rev. 6/96

ORIGINAL ORATION

Section 1. An original oration shall be defined as a memorized, original persuasive speech with an unique approach to an universal theme.

Sec. 2. Original orations shall be the work of the student.

    a. If a student qualifies for regional or state speech and drama festival or state speech championship, and it is found he/she has been guilty of plagiarism, he/she shall be disqualified. Plagiarism shall be defined as a quotation of more than four words without giving the source.

    b. Students should be encouraged to use standard persuasive format; such as, Monroe's Motivated Sequence (Attention, Need, Satisfaction, Visualization, Action) or Problem-Cause-Solution.

Sec. 3. Original orations shall not be more than ten (10) minutes in length.

Sec. 4. Original orations shall be memorized and given without notes. Prompting shall not be allowed. Charts, displays, maps, graphs or any other materials which could be used for demonstration purposes **are not permissible.**

TIME PENALTIES

1. Performances in all individual events shall be within set time limits for each event.

2. If an **official timekeeper** is present, the following shall occur:

    a. Time shall be **visible** to the performer(s). (Time cards or similar procedures may be used.)

    b. After the "STOP" card goes up, there shall be a 15-second grace period. Upon completion of the additional 15 seconds, the time-keeper shall stand and keep timing until the performer(s) is finished.

    c. Any performance in excess of the 15-second grace period shall not receive the First Division rating or the "I" ranking in the round.

3. If no official timekeeper is present, no penalty shall be enforced. **THE JUDGE SHALL NOT SERVE AS OFFICIAL TIMEKEEPER.**

JUDGE'S COMMENTS

KANSAS STATE HIGH SCHOOL ACTIVITIES ASSOCIATION
SPEECH & DRAMA INVITATIONALS, FESTIVALS & CHAMPIONSHIPS

ORAL INTERPRETATION *(Reading of Prose)*

NAME and/or CODE # _____   SCHOOL and/or CODE # _____

SELECTION _____   ROUND _____   ROOM _____

Judge's Signature _____

Please write judge's comments on the back of this ballot.
Remember, this is to be a learning experience.

Oral Interpretation of Prose is divided into two sections:

1. The participant shall give a brief introduction to his/her selection or selections.

2. He/she shall read one or more selections from the printed manuscript.

Choice of Selections

A. Do the selections fit the reader's personality and capabilities?

B. Do the selections have sufficient literary merit to warrant study and practice for interpretation before a group?

Adequacy of Introduction

A. Does the introduction give sufficient information to establish the proper mood and understanding on the part of the student?

B. Does it arouse attention and interest?

C. Was the transition from the introduction to the selection done effectively and smoothly?

Comprehension of Selections

A. Does the reader respond emotionally to the thought and mood?

B. Does he/she understand theme, purpose and author's point of view?

Comprehension of Selections *continued*

C. Does he/she understand intent of unusual words and figures of speech?

D. Does he/she emphasize the words and phrases on which the humor or drama of the selections depends?

Audience Contact

A. Is the reader well poised?

B. Does he/she exhibit genuine desire to communicate with his/her audience?

C. Are his/her face and body responsive to the mood of the selection?

Voice and Diction

A. Is the reader's voice adequate, pleasant and responsive to the meaning of the selection?

B. Is the pronunciation acceptable?

C. Is the enunciation distinct without being pedantic?

Time Limit: Entrants exceeding the seven-minute time limit shall be penalized as indicated on the reverse side. Students may complete last sentence. *(Please indicate if excessive time applies.)* There is no minimum time requirement.

Participant's Information: Please remember that the sections of your ballot do not carry equal weight. Each judge is allowed to determine the percentage evaluation of each section.

KSHSAA SPEECH & DRAMA
INVITATIONALS—FESTIVALS—CHAMPIONSHIPS

RANK CONTESTANTS CONSECUTIVELY (1st = BEST)
Circle **ONE RANK ONLY**. *No two contestants may receive the same rank.*

1st   2nd   3rd   4th   5th   6th   7th   8th   9th   10th

Circle **ONE NUMBER ONLY** (25 = BEST) for **QUALITY POINTS** or **TOURNAMENT RATING**
Contestants may receive the same quality points or tournament rating.

25 24 23 22 21   20 19 18 17 16   15 14 13 12 11   10 9 8 7 6

SPEECH & DRAMA FESTIVALS
Circle **ONE ROMAN NUMERAL** (I = BEST) for **DIVISION RATING**

I   II   III   IV

NOTE: These are available from the KSHSAA. See order blank in *KSHSAA Speech and Drama Manual*

(OVER)

Rev. 6/96

ORAL INTERPRETATION OF PROSE

Section 1. Prose expresses thought through language recorded in sentences and paragraphs. Prose includes fiction (short stories, novels) and non-fiction (articles, essays, journals, biographies). No play scripts or other material in script form may be used.

Sec. 2. Time: Presentations shall not last more than seven (7) minutes including a required introduction which will state at least the title(s) and author(s). The introduction must be memorized. The participant may complete a sentence after time is called. If an official timekeeper is assigned, a participant shall be penalized if the time limit is exceeded.

Sec. 3. Selection: One or more selections of prose shall be **read from the printed manuscript** during the performance.

    a. "Printed" shall be interpreted to mean either the printed manuscript or a typewritten copy.

    b. Only published printed words may be used. No play scripts or other material in script form may be used. In the event of a challenge of material, the coach or sponsor must supply proof of the publication of the material.

    c. The selection or selections shall NOT be memorized.

    d. Selections shall be made by the student and prepared before the tournament.

    e. No properties shall be allowed.

Sec. 4. Presentation: Performances must be from a manuscript (which may be in a folder). Reading from a book or magazine is not permitted. Since the contestant will be holding a manuscript, use of that manuscript should be an integral part of the performance. Responsive use of the body (i.e., spontaneous changes in posture and gesture) is permissible so long as this active use of the body is appropriate to the demands of the selection and a natural outgrowth from the literature being performed. With the exception of a small step at transitions, the performer's feet shall not move. Along with appropriate, effective physical presentation, the contestant will also be evaluated in terms of technique (breathing, tone, pitch, enunciation, phrasing, pace, etc.) and artistry (presentation of mood and imagery, vocal characterization, etc.). The final test of good interpretation is the ability to use all these factors so successfully and unobtrusively that the audience forgets that this is a contest in a created atmosphere and is carried into the real or imagined world of the selection(s).

TIME PENALTIES

1. Performances in all individual events shall be within set time limits for each event.

2. If an **official timekeeper** is present, the following shall occur:

    a. Time shall be **visible** to the performer(s). (Time cards or similar procedures may be used.)

    b. After the "STOP" card goes up, there shall be a 15-second grace period. Upon completion of the additional 15 seconds, the timekeeper shall stand and keep timing until the performer(s) is finished.

    c. Any performance in excess of the 15-second grace period shall not receive the First Division rating or the "I" ranking in the round.

3. If no official timekeeper is present, no penalty shall be enforced. **THE JUDGE SHALL NOT SERVE AS OFFICIAL TIMEKEEPER.**

JUDGE'S COMMENTS

KANSAS STATE HIGH SCHOOL ACTIVITIES ASSOCIATION
SPEECH & DRAMA INVITATIONALS, FESTIVALS & CHAMPIONSHIPS

ORAL INTERPRETATION *(Reading of Poetry)*

NAME and/or CODE # _____   SCHOOL and/or CODE # _____

SELECTION _____   ROUND _____   ROOM _____

Judge's Signature _____

Please write judge's comments on the back of this ballot.
Remember, this is to be a learning experience.

Oral Interpretation of Poetry is divided into two sections:

1. The participant shall give a brief introduction to his/her selection or selections.
2. He/she shall read one or more selections from the printed manuscript.

Choice of Selections

A. Do the selections fit the reader's personality and capabilities?

B. Do the selections have sufficient literary merit to warrant study and practice for interpretation before a group?

Adequacy of Introduction

A. Does the introduction give sufficient information to establish the proper mood and understanding on the part of the student?

B. Does it arouse attention and interest?

C. Was the transition from the introduction to the selection done effectively and smoothly?

Comprehension of Selections

A. Does the reader respond emotionally to the thought and mood?

B. Does he/she understand theme, purpose and author's point of view?

Comprehension of Selections *continued*

C. Does he/she understand intent of unusual words and figures of speech?

D. Does he/she emphasize the words and phrases on which the humor or drama of the selections depends?

Audience Contact

A. Is the reader well poised?

B. Does he/she exhibit genuine desire to communicate with his/her audience?

C. Are his/her face and body responsive to the mood of the selection?

Voice and Diction

A. Is the reader's voice adequate, pleasant and responsive to the meaning of the selection?

B. Is the pronunciation acceptable?

C. Is the enunciation distinct without being pedantic?

Time Limit: Entrants exceeding the seven-minute time limit shall be penalized as indicated on the reverse side. Students may complete last sentence. *(Please indicate if excessive time applies.)* There is no minimum time requirement.

Participant's Information: Please remember that the sections of your ballot do not carry equal weight. Each judge is allowed to determine the percentage evaluation of each section.

KSHSAA SPEECH & DRAMA
INVITATIONALS—FESTIVALS—CHAMPIONSHIPS

RANK CONTESTANTS CONSECUTIVELY (1st = BEST)
Circle **ONE RANK ONLY**. *No two contestants may receive the same rank.*

1st   2nd   3rd   4th   5th   6th   7th   8th   9th   10th

Circle **ONE NUMBER ONLY** (25 = BEST) for **QUALITY POINTS** or **TOURNAMENT RATING**
Contestants may receive the same quality points or tournament rating.

25 24 23 22 21   20 19 18 17 16   15 14 13 12 11   10 9 8 7 6

SPEECH & DRAMA FESTIVALS
Circle **ONE ROMAN NUMERAL** (I = BEST) for **DIVISION RATING**

I   II   III   IV

NOTE: These are available from the KSHSAA. See order blank in *KSHSAA Speech and Drama Manual*
(OVER)

Rev. 6/96

ORAL INTERPRETATION OF POETRY

Section 1. Poetry is writing which expresses ideas, experience or emotion through the creative arrangement of words according to their sound, their rhythm and their meaning. Poetry relies on verse and stanza form.

Sec. 2. Time: Presentations shall not last more than seven (7) minutes including required introduction which will state at least the title(s) and author(s). The introduction must be memorized. The participant may complete a sentence after time is called. If an official timekeeper is assigned, a participant shall be penalized if the time limit is exceeded.

Sec. 3. Selection: One or more selections of poetry shall be **read from the printed manuscript** during the performance.

    a. "Printed" shall be interpreted to mean either the printed manuscript or a typewritten copy.

    b. Only published printed words may be used. No play scripts or other material in script form may be used. In the event of a challenge of material, the coach or sponsor must supply proof of the publication of the material.

    c. The selection or selections shall NOT be memorized.

    d. Selections shall be made by the student and prepared before the tournament.

    e. No properties shall be allowed.

Sec. 4. Presentation: Performances must be from a manuscript (which may be in a folder). Reading from a book or magazine is not permitted. Since the contestant will be holding a manuscript, use of that manuscript should be an integral part of the performance. Responsive use of the body (i.e., spontaneous changes in posture and gesture) is permissible so long as this active use of the body is appropriate to the demands of the selection and a natural outgrowth from the literature being performed. With the exception of a small step at transitions, the performer's feet shall not move. Along with appropriate, effective physical presentation, the contestant will also be evaluated in terms of technique (breathing, tone, pitch, enunciation, phrasing, pace, etc.) and artistry (presentation of mood and imagery, vocal characterization, etc.). The final test of good interpretation is the ability to use all these factors so successfully and unobtrusively that the audience forgets that this is a contest in a created atmosphere and is carried into the real or imagined world of the selection(s).

TIME PENALTIES

1. Performances in all individual events shall be within set time limits for each event.

2. If an **official timekeeper** is present, the following shall occur:

    a. Time shall be **visible** to the performer(s). (Time cards or similar procedures may be used.)

    b. After the "STOP" card goes up, there shall be a 15-second grace period. Upon completion of the additional 15 seconds, the timekeeper shall stand and keep timing until the performer(s) is finished.

    c. Any performance in excess of the 15-second grace period shall not receive the First Division rating or the "I" ranking in the round.

3. If no official timekeeper is present, no penalty shall be enforced. **THE JUDGE SHALL NOT SERVE AS OFFICIAL TIMEKEEPER.**

JUDGE'S COMMENTS

KANSAS STATE HIGH SCHOOL ACTIVITIES ASSOCIATION
SPEECH & DRAMA INVITATIONALS, FESTIVALS & CHAMPIONSHIPS

SOLO ACTING *(Serious)*

NAME and/or CODE # _____   SCHOOL and/or CODE # _____

SELECTION _____   ROUND _____   ROOM _____

Judge's Signature _____

Please write judge's comments on the back of this ballot.
Remember, this is to be a learning experience.

Choice of Selection

A. Is the selection appropriate for the actor's ability?

B. Is the drama of the selection suitable for festival presentation?

Comprehension of the Selection

A. Does the actor respond emotionally to the thought and mood?

B. Is the theme, purpose and point of view of the author understood by the actor?

C. Is the intent of unusual words and figures of speech understood?

D. Are the words and phrases on which the drama of the selection depends, emphasized?

Audience Contact

A. Is the actor well poised?

B. Does the actor exhibit a genuine desire to communicate with the audience?

C. Are face and body responsive to the mood of the selection?

Voice and Diction

A. Is the actor's voice adequate, pleasant and responsive to the meaning of the selection?

B. Is the pronunciation acceptable?

C. Is the enunciation distinct without being pedantic?

Characterization

A. Is the character delineation vivid and consistent?

B. Are movements motivated?

Time Limit: Entrants exceeding the ten-minute time limit shall be penalized as indicated on the reverse side. Students may complete last sentence. *(Please indicate if excessive time applies.)* There is no minimum time requirement.

Participant's Information: Please remember that the sections of your ballot do not carry equal weight. Each judge is allowed to determine the percentage evaluation of each section.

KSHSAA SPEECH & DRAMA
INVITATIONALS—FESTIVALS—CHAMPIONSHIPS

RANK CONTESTANTS CONSECUTIVELY (1st = BEST)
Circle **ONE RANK ONLY.** *No two contestants may receive the same rank.*

1st   2nd   3rd   4th   5th   6th   7th   8th   9th   10th

Circle **ONE NUMBER ONLY** (25 = BEST) for **QUALITY POINTS** or **TOURNAMENT RATING**
Contestants may receive the same quality points or tournament rating.

25 24 23 22 21   20 19 18 17 16   15 14 13 12 11   10 9 8 7 6

SPEECH & DRAMA FESTIVALS
Circle **ONE ROMAN NUMERAL** (I = BEST) for **DIVISION RATING**

I   II   III   IV

NOTE: These are available from the KSHSAA. See order blank in *KSHSAA Speech and Drama Manual*

(OVER)

Rev. 6/96

SAMPLE

SERIOUS SOLO ACTING

Section 1. Serious Solo Acting shall not be more than ten (10) minutes in length including an introduction. A student may participate and qualify in both serious and humorous solo acting categories.

Sec. 2. Serious Solo Acting selections shall be **memorized** and given without notes. Prompting shall not be allowed.

Sec. 3. Serious Solo Acting shall be interpreted as an acting event where the entire stage area may be used. Stage properties and costumes shall be prohibited with the exception of a chair.

Sec. 4. The actor should use only actions motivated by the language/characterization of the selection.

Sec. 5. A person who qualifies in Dramatic Interpretation is eligible for Serious Solo Acting at state speech championship and state speech and drama festival. (The event sponsored by KSHSAA is solo acting. However, some tournaments use dramatic and humorous interpretations which limits movement and action more than the acting event.)

Sec. 6. Selections shall be taken from published works of serious literature and shall **NOT** be taken from records or tapes, television or movies or be the original work of the student or coach. Selections can include play scripts, short stories, novels and poetry. In the event of a challenge of material, the coach or sponsor must supply proof of the publication of the material.

TIME PENALTIES

1. Performances in all individual events shall be within set time limits for each event.

2. If an **official timekeeper** is present, the following shall occur:

   a. Time shall be **visible** to the performer(s). (Time cards or similar procedures may be used.)

   b. After the "STOP" card goes up, there shall be a 15-second grace period. Upon completion of the additional 15 seconds, the time-keeper shall stand and keep timing until the performer(s) is finished.

   c. Any performance in excess of the 15-second grace period shall not receive the First Division rating or the "I" ranking in the round.

3. If no official timekeeper is present, no penalty shall be enforced. **THE JUDGE SHALL NOT SERVE AS OFFICIAL TIMEKEEPER.**

JUDGE'S COMMENTS

SAMPLE

KANSAS STATE HIGH SCHOOL ACTIVITIES ASSOCIATION
SPEECH & DRAMA INVITATIONALS, FESTIVALS & CHAMPIONSHIPS

SOLO ACTING *(Humorous)*

NAME and/or CODE # _____   SCHOOL and/or CODE # _____

SELECTION _____   ROUND _____   ROOM _____

Judge's Signature _____

Please write judge's comments on the back of this ballot.
Remember, this is to be a learning experience.

Choice of Selection

  A. Is the selection appropriate for the actor's ability?

  B. Is the humor of the selection suitable for festival presentation?

Comprehension of the Selection

  A. Does the actor respond emotionally to the thought and mood?

  B. Is the theme, purpose and point of view of the author understood by the actor?

  C. Is the intent of unusual words and figures of speech understood?

  D. Are the words and phrases on which the humor of the selection depends, emphasized?

Audience Contact

  A. Is the actor well poised?

  B. Does the actor exhibit a genuine desire to communicate with the audience?

  C. Are face and body responsive to the mood of the selection?

Voice and Diction

  A. Is the actor's voice adequate, pleasant and responsive to the meaning of the selection?

  B. Is the pronunciation acceptable?

  C. Is the enunciation distinct without being pedantic?

Characterization

  A. Is the character delineation vivid and consistent?

  B. Are movements motivated?

Time Limit: Entrants exceeding the ten-minute time limit shall be penalized as indicated on the reverse side. Students may complete last sentence. *(Please indicate if excessive time applies.)* There is no minimum time requirement.

Participant's Information: Please remember that the sections of your ballot do not carry equal weight. Each judge is allowed to determine the percentage evaluation of each section.

KSHSAA SPEECH & DRAMA
INVITATIONALS—FESTIVALS—CHAMPIONSHIPS

RANK CONTESTANTS CONSECUTIVELY (1st = BEST)
Circle **ONE RANK ONLY**. *No two contestants may receive the same rank.*

  1st   2nd   3rd   4th   5th   6th   7th   8th   9th   10th

Circle **ONE NUMBER ONLY** (25 = BEST) for **QUALITY POINTS** or **TOURNAMENT RATING**
Contestants may receive the same quality points or tournament rating.

25 24 23 22 21   20 19 18 17 16   15 14 13 12 11   10 9 8 7 6

SPEECH & DRAMA FESTIVALS
Circle **ONE ROMAN NUMERAL** (I = BEST) for **DIVISION RATING**

    I   II   III   IV

NOTE: These are available from the KSHSAA. See order blank in *KSHSAA Speech and Drama Manual*

(OVER)

Rev. 6/96

HUMOROUS SOLO ACTING

Section 1. Humorous Solo Acting shall not be more than ten (10) minutes in length including an introduction. A student may participate and qualify in both serious and humorous solo acting categories.

Sec. 2. Humorous Solo Acting selections shall be **memorized** and given without notes. Prompting shall not be allowed.

Sec. 3. Humorous Solo Acting shall be interpreted as an acting event where the entire stage area may be used. Stage properties and costumes shall be prohibited with the exception of a chair.

Sec. 4. The actor should use only actions motivated by the language/characterization of the selection.

Sec. 5. A person who qualifies in Humorous Interpretation is eligible for Humorous Solo Acting at state speech championship and state speech and drama festival. (The event sponsored by KSHSAA is solo acting. However, some tournaments use dramatic and humorous interpretations which limits movement and action more than the acting event.)

Sec. 6. Selections shall be taken from published works of humorous literature and shall **NOT** be taken from records or tapes, television or movies or be the original work of the student or coach. Selections can include play scripts, short stories, novels and poetry. In the event of a challenge of material, the coach or sponsor must supply proof of the publication of the material.

TIME PENALTIES

1. Performances in all individual events shall be within set time limits for each event.

2. If an **official timekeeper** is present, the following shall occur:

   a. Time shall be **visible** to the performer(s). (Time cards or similar procedures may be used.)

   b. After the "STOP" card goes up, there shall be a 15-second grace period. Upon completion of the additional 15 seconds, the timekeeper shall stand and keep timing until the performer(s) is finished.

   c. Any performance in excess of the 15-second grace period shall not receive the First Division rating or the "I" ranking in the round.

3. If no official timekeeper is present, no penalty shall be enforced. **THE JUDGE SHALL NOT SERVE AS OFFICIAL TIMEKEEPER.**

JUDGE'S COMMENTS

KANSAS STATE HIGH SCHOOL ACTIVITIES ASSOCIATION
SPEECH & DRAMA INVITATIONALS, FESTIVALS & CHAMPIONSHIPS
DUET ACTING

"Duet Acting shall be defined as an acting exercise composed of two students who portray a memorized ten-minute cutting from a published work of literature." — *KSHSAA Speech and Drama Manual*

NAME and/or CODE # _____ NAME and/or CODE # _____ ROUND

SCHOOL and/or CODE # _____ SELECTION _____ ROOM

SAMPLE

Judge's Signature _____

Please write judge's comments on the back of this ballot.
Remember, this is to be a learning experience.

Selction of Material

A. Is the cutting a good vehicle for acting?

B. Is the cutting well planned and well executed?

C. Are the introductions and transitions effective?

D. Does it have continuity? Build to a climax?

Direction

A. Is the movement well planned?

B. Is the relationship between characters clearly defined?

C. Does the presentation have tempo and rhythm appropriate to the scene?

D. Is the cutting suitably cast?

Acting

A. Does the individual actor have a distinct characterization, projected both physically and mentally?

B. Is he/she sincere? Is he/she believable?

C. Do the two actors act and react to each other?

D. Are the actors audible and articulate?

Dramatic Effectiveness

A. Did the scene create an illusion?

B. How effectively did the performers overcome the absence of costumes, props, make-up and setting?

C. Did the performance create an empathic response?

Time Limit: Entrants exceeding the ten-minute time limit shall be penalized as indicated on the reverse side. Students may complete last sentence. *(Please indicate if excessive time applies.)* There is no minimum time requirement.

Participant's Information: Please remember that the sections of your ballot do not carry equal weight. Each judge is allowed to determine the percentage evaluation of each section.

KSHSAA SPEECH & DRAMA
INVITATIONALS—FESTIVALS—CHAMPIONSHIPS

RANK CONTESTANTS CONSECUTIVELY (1st = BEST)
Circle **ONE RANK ONLY**. *No two contestants may receive the same rank.*

1st   2nd   3rd   4th   5th   6th   7th   8th   9th   10th

Circle **ONE NUMBER ONLY** (25 = BEST) for **QUALITY POINTS** or **TOURNAMENT RATING**
Contestants may receive the same quality points or tournament rating.

25 24 23 22 21   20 19 18 17 16   15 14 13 12 11   10 9 8 7 6

SPEECH & DRAMA FESTIVALS
Circle **ONE ROMAN NUMERAL** (I = BEST) for **DIVISION RATING**

I   II   III   IV

NOTE: These are available from the KSHSAA. See order blank in *KSHSAA Speech and Drama Manual*

(OVER)

Rev. 6/96

DUET ACTING (DA)

Section 1. Duet Acting shall be defined as an acting exercise composed of two students who portray a memorized ten (10)-minute cutting from a published work of literature. Prompting shall not be allowed.

Sec. 2. Duet acting selections shall not be more than ten minutes in length. This shall include the introduction.

Sec. 3. A student shall portray only one character in a scene. **However, he/she may portray more than one character if the cutting consists of more than one scene, or if the scene is written for the actors' portrayal of multiple characters.** Cuttings of multiple scenes must be bridged by memorized narration.

Sec. 4. A narrated introduction to the cutting shall be given by one or both members. This shall be included in the ten (10)-minute time limit.

Sec. 5. Stage make-up, costumes or properties shall be prohibited with the exception of two (2) chairs and a table.

Sec. 6. Selections shall be taken from published works of humorous or dramatic literature and shall NOT be taken from records or tapes, television or movies, or be the original work of the student or coach. Selections can include play scripts, short stories, novels and poetry. In the event of a challenge of material, the coach or sponsor must supply proof of the publication of the material.

TIME PENALTIES

1. Performances in all individual events shall be within set time limits for each event.

2. If an **official timekeeper** is present, the following shall occur:

   a. Time shall be **visible** to the performer(s). (Time cards or similar procedures may be used.)

   b. After the "STOP" card goes up, there shall be a 15-second grace period. Upon completion of the additional 15 seconds, the time-keeper shall stand and keep timing until the performer(s) is finished.

   c. Any performance in excess of the 15-second grace period shall not receive the First Division rating or the "I" ranking in the round.

3. If no official timekeeper is present, no penalty shall be enforced. **THE JUDGE SHALL NOT SERVE AS OFFICIAL TIMEKEEPER.**

JUDGE'S COMMENTS

KANSAS STATE HIGH SCHOOL ACTIVITIES ASSOCIATION
SPEECH & DRAMA INVITATIONALS, FESTIVALS & CHAMPIONSHIPS

IMPROVISED DUET ACTING

"Improvised duet acting shall be defined as an improvised acting exercise composed of two students who portray an original scene created after drawing the subject. The scene should establish two characters, a situation or problem and a solution to the conflict." — KSHSAA Speech and Drama Manual

NAME and/or CODE # _____   NAME and/or CODE # _____   ROUND _____

SCHOOL and/or CODE # _____   SELECTION _____   ROOM _____

Judge's Signature _____

Please write judge's comments on the back of this ballot.
Remember, this is to be a learning experience.

Completeness of Scene

A. Was the scene set up with an introduction?

B. Does the scene have continuity? Does it build to a climax?

C. Does the scene have a beginning, middle and an end?

D. Does the scene develop the topic drawn?

Direction

A. Is the movement well planned or contrived?

B. Is the relationship between characters clearly defined?

C. Does the presentation have tempo and rhythm appropriate to the scene?

Dialogue

A. Did it seem natural or contrived?

B. Did it move the plot or conflict toward a climax?

C. Is it original? Meaningful?

Dialogue *continued*

D. Do the actors speak with energy and meaning?

E. Was dialogue appropriate to their characters?

Acting

A. Do the individual actors have a distinct characterization, projected both physically and mentally?

B. Are they sincere? Are they believable?

C. Do the two actors act and react to each other?

Dramatic Effectiveness

A. How effectively did the performers overcome the absence of costumes, props, make-up and setting?

B. Did the performance create an empathic response?

C. Was the scene clever and imaginative?

Time Limit: Entrants exceeding the seven-minute time limit *(minimum four minutes)* shall be penalized as indicated on the reverse side. Students may complete last sentence. *(Please indicate if time penalties apply.)*

Participant's Information: Please remember that the sections of your ballot do not carry equal weight. Each judge is allowed to determine the percentage evaluation of each section.

KSHSAA SPEECH & DRAMA
INVITATIONALS—FESTIVALS—CHAMPIONSHIPS

RANK CONTESTANTS CONSECUTIVELY (1st = BEST)
Circle **ONE RANK ONLY.** *No two contestants may receive the same rank.*

1st   2nd   3rd   4th   5th   6th   7th   8th   9th   10th

Circle **ONE NUMBER ONLY** (25 = BEST) for **QUALITY POINTS** or **TOURNAMENT RATING**
Contestants may receive the same quality points or tournament rating.

25   24   23   22   21   20   19   18   17   16   15   14   13   12   11   10   9   8   7   6

SPEECH & DRAMA FESTIVALS
Circle **ONE ROMAN NUMERAL** (I = BEST) for **DIVISION RATING**

I   II   III   IV

NOTE: These are available from the KSHSAA. See order blank in *KSHSAA Speech and Drama Manual*
(OVER)   Rev. 6/96

IMPROVISED DUET ACTING (IDA)

Section 1. Improvised duet acting shall be defined as an improvised acting exercise composed of two students who portray an **original scene** created after drawing the subject. The scene should establish two characters, a situation or problem and a solution to the conflict.

Sec. 2. Topics

a. **Drawing:** Each IDA team shall draw three (3) topics from EACH of the following areas: **character**, **situation** and **location**. There shall be ONE topic on each slip of paper. From the items drawn, each IDA team shall choose two (2) characters, one (1) situation and one (1) location. The remaining topics shall be returned.

Topics should be "generic" in nature which require **improvisation** and not **impersonation**. For example, proper nouns would not be appropriate topics.

b. **Preparation:** The drawings for topics shall be held in a room apart from the preparation room. The chairperson of the preparation room shall be instructed to allow no visitors (or coaches) and to keep students from discussing their topic with others. Actors may not consult either printed matter, notes, manuscripts or other media.

c. **Time Limit:** Each IDA team shall have 30 minutes to prepare.

Sec. 3. Improvised duet acting shall not be more than seven (7) minutes in length with a minimum of four (4) minutes. This shall include the introduction. If an official timekeeper is assigned, participants shall be penalized if the time limits are not observed.

Sec. 4. An actor may portray only one character throughout the seven (7) minute presentation. No additional characters can be used for the introduction. If an official timekeeper is assigned, participants shall be penalized if the time limits are not observed.

Sec. 5. A brief narrated introduction shall be used in establishing the setting and the characters in the scene.

Sec. 6. All dialogue must be the original work of the contestants.

Sec. 7. Stage properties or costumes shall be prohibited with the exception of two (2) chairs and a table.

Sec. 8. Students shall not repeat nor copy any scene they have previously performed at that tournament. **A repeated scene is defined as a repetition of dialogue, character(s) and conflict structure (This means an IDA team must repeat all three (3) elements to be in violation of this rule).**

Sec. 9. Any schools wishing to experiment with various formats in this event may do so as long as the tournament invitation expresses the regulations governing this experimentation. **No students entered in this experimental event may qualify for state festival or state championship competition.**

TIME PENALTIES

1. Performances in all individual events shall be within set time limits for each event.

2. If an **official timekeeper** is present, the following shall occur:

a. Time shall be **visible** to the performer(s). (Time cards or similar procedures may be used.)

b. After the "STOP" card goes up, there shall be a 15-second grace period. Upon completion of the additional 15 seconds, the time-keeper shall stand and keep timing until the performer(s) is finished.

c. Any performance in excess of the 15-second grace period shall not receive the First Division rating or the "I" ranking in the round.

d. Any performance under the four-minute minimum time limit in Improvised Duet Acting shall not receive the First Division rating or the "I" ranking in the round.

3. If no official timekeeper is present, no penalty shall be enforced. **THE JUDGE SHALL NOT SERVE AS OFFICIAL TIMEKEEPER.**

JUDGE'S COMMENTS

KANSAS STATE HIGH SCHOOL ACTIVITIES ASSOCIATION
SPEECH & DRAMA INVITATIONALS, FESTIVALS & CHAMPIONSHIPS

EXTEMPORANEOUS SPEECH

"The extemporaneous speech is a spontaneous, original oral expression of ideas on a given subject about which the speaker has had previous knowledge, preparation and planning. The speech is never memorized." — *KSHSAA Speech and Drama Manual*

NAME and/or CODE # _____   SCHOOL and/or CODE # _____

TOPIC _____   ROUND _____   ROOM _____

Judge's Signature _____

**Please write judge's comments on the back of this ballot.
Remember, this is to be a learning experience.**

Adhere to Subject

A. Was the speech a reasonable development of the exact topic selected?

Information

A. Does the speaker give support of his/her ideas with factual examples and illustrations?

B. Does he/she use the information to develop his/her ideas?

Organization

A. Does the speaker present the introduction and conclusion in an adequate manner?

B. Does the speaker make his/her points and transitions in an adequate manner?

Diction

A. Does the speaker use language that is appropriate, colorful and exact?

B. Does the speaker pronounce and enunciate his/her words in a satisfactory manner?

Delivery

A. Is the speaker direct, animated and communicative in manner?

Time Limit: Entrants exceeding the seven-minute time limit shall be penalized as indicated on the reverse side. Students may complete last sentence. *(Please indicate if excessive time applies.)* There is no minimum time requirement.

Participant's Information: Please remember that the sections of your ballot do not carry equal weight. Each judge is allowed to determine the percentage evaluation of each section.

KSHSAA SPEECH & DRAMA
INVITATIONALS—FESTIVALS—CHAMPIONSHIPS

RANK CONTESTANTS CONSECUTIVELY (1st = BEST)
Circle **ONE RANK ONLY**. *No two contestants may receive the same rank.*

1st   2nd   3rd   4th   5th   6th   7th   8th   9th   10th

Circle **ONE NUMBER ONLY** (25 = BEST) for **QUALITY POINTS** or **TOURNAMENT RATING**
Contestants may receive the same quality points or tournament rating.

25 24 23 22 21   20 19 18 17 16   15 14 13 12 11   10 9 8 7 6

SPEECH & DRAMA FESTIVALS
Circle **ONE ROMAN NUMERAL** (I = BEST) for **DIVISION RATING**

I   II   III   IV

NOTE: These are available from the KSHSAA. See order blank in *KSHSAA Speech and Drama Manual*

(OVER)   Rev. 6/96

EXTEMPORANEOUS SPEECH

Section 1. The extemporaneous speech is a spontaneous, original oral expression of ideas on a given subject about which the speaker has had previous knowledge, preparation and planning. The speech is never memorized.

Topics:

The general subject for extemporaneous speech shall be "Current Affairs." Topics shall cover both domestic and foreign affairs. Specifically, U.S. domestic **and** U.S. foreign policy (domestic affairs); and domestic affairs of foreign countries and the foreign affairs of all countries, including the United States (foreign affairs). The topics shall be worded in question form and be selected from *Time, U.S. News & World Report,* and *Newsweek.* Topics shall be selected from issues published between **December 1** and **April 1** of the current school year.

a. The topics shall be used in regional and state speech and drama festivals and shall be supplied by the KSHSAA.

b. The topics shall be used in state speech championships and shall be supplied by the KSHSAA.

c. At state speech championships and regional and state speech and drama festivals, there shall be two topic divisions: Domestic and Foreign. Students may draw from either division.

Sec. 2. Drawing: Each participant shall draw three topics, choose one and return the other two. The other participants shall draw in like manner, in the order of speaking, at intervals of ten minutes. A participant drawing a topic on which she/he has spoken previously in the tournament shall return it and draw again.

Sec. 3. Preparation: As soon as a topic is chosen, the participant shall withdraw and prepare a speech without consultation and without references to prepared notes. Students may consult originals or photocopies of published books, magazines, newspapers, journals, articles or **unannotated indices.**

No other material shall be allowed in the extemporaneous prep room. Extemporaneous speeches, handbooks, briefs and outlines shall be barred from the extemporaneous prep room. Underlining or highlighting will be allowed if done in only one color on each article or copy. No electrical retrieval device may be used. There shall be a full 30 minutes of preparation time for each student. Students are not allowed to consult other individuals and shall remain in the extemporaneous preparation room the full 30 minutes.

Sec. 4. Notes: During the speech, brief notes **may be** used but they must on a single card no larger than a 4 x 6 note card. The judge is expected to enforce this rule. The ethics committee shall decide on the penalty of disqualification for the use of more copious notes.

Sec. 5. Time: The extemporaneous speech shall be no longer than seven (7) minutes.

TIME PENALTIES

1. Performances in all individual events shall be within set time limits for each event.

2. If an **official timekeeper** is present, the following shall occur:

a. Time shall be **visible** to the performer(s). (Time cards or similar procedures may be used.)

b. After the "STOP" card goes up, there shall be a 15-second grace period. Upon completion of the additional 15 seconds, the timekeeper shall stand and keep timing until the performer(s) is finished.

c. Any performance in excess of the 15-second grace period shall not receive the First Division rating or the "I" ranking in the round.

3. If no official timekeeper is present, no penalty shall be enforced. **THE JUDGE SHALL NOT SERVE AS OFFICIAL TIMEKEEPER.**

JUDGE'S COMMENTS

KANSAS STATE HIGH SCHOOL ACTIVITIES ASSOCIATION
SPEECH & DRAMA INVITATIONALS, FESTIVALS & CHAMPIONSHIPS

INFORMATIVE SPEECH

"An informative speech is one which provides a learning experience for the listener by instructing or giving information in an interesting manner." — *KSHSAA Speech and Drama Manual*

NAME and/or CODE # _____   SCHOOL and/or CODE # _____

TITLE _____   ROUND _____   ROOM _____

Judge's Signature _____

Please write judge's comments on the back of this ballot.
Remember, this is to be a learning experience.

Selection of Subject

   A. Does the subject allow the speaker to present new information in an interesting manner?

   B. Is there opportunity for adequate use of examples and illustrations to clarify the major points in the speech?

Organization of Material

   A. Does the speaker include the most significant materials available in his/her speech?

   B. Are these materials so arranged as to be most effective?

   C. Does the speaker reveal the development of an appropriate organizing principle?

Diction

   A. Is the language of the speaker suitable, colorful and vivid?

   B. Is the voice pleasant, with enough variety and emphasis?

   C. Does the speaker employ proper pronunciation and effective enunciation?

Delivery

   A. Is the speaker poised, animated and directly vocal and physically communicative?

   B. Does he/she have distracting habits and mannerisms?

SAMPLE

Time Limit: Entrants exceeding the seven-minute time limit shall be penalized as indicated on the reverse side. Students may complete last sentence. *(Please indicate if excessive time applies.)* There is no minimum time requirement.

Participant's Information: Please remember that the sections of your ballot do not carry equal weight. Each judge is allowed to determine the percentage evaluation of each section.

KSHSAA SPEECH & DRAMA
INVITATIONALS—FESTIVALS—CHAMPIONSHIPS

RANK CONTESTANTS CONSECUTIVELY (1st = BEST)
Circle **ONE RANK ONLY**. *No two contestants may receive the same rank.*

   1st   2nd   3rd   4th   5th   6th   7th   8th   9th   10th

Circle **ONE NUMBER ONLY** (25 = BEST) for **QUALITY POINTS** or **TOURNAMENT RATING**
Contestants may receive the same quality points or tournament rating.

25 24 23 22 21   20 19 18 17 16   15 14 13 12 11   10 9 8 7 6

SPEECH & DRAMA FESTIVALS
Circle **ONE ROMAN NUMERAL** (I = BEST) for **DIVISION RATING**

   I   II   III   IV

NOTE: These are available from the KSHSAA. See order blank in *KSHSAA Speech and Drama Manual*
(OVER)

Rev. 6/96

INFORMATIVE SPEECH

Section 1. An informative speech is one which provides a learning experience for the listener by instructing or by giving information in an interesting manner.

Sec. 2. Informative speeches shall be the work of the student.

    a. If a student qualifies for regional or state speech and drama festival or state speech championship, and it is found he/she has been guilty of plagiarism, he/she shall be disqualified. Plagiarism shall be defined as a quotation of more than four words without giving the source.

    b. Students should be encouraged to use good informative format: Introduction (attention device, sign-posting/preview of topics, etc.), Body and Conclusion.

Sec. 3. Speeches shall not be more than seven (7) minutes in length.

Sec. 4. Informative speeches shall be memorized and given without notes. Prompting shall not be allowed. Charts, displays, maps, graphs or any other materials which could be used for demonstration purposed **are not permissible.**

TIME PENALTIES

1. Performances in all individual events shall be within set time limits for each event.

2. If an **official timekeeper** is present, the following shall occur:

    a. Time shall be **visible** to the performer(s). (Time cards or similar procedures may be used.)

    b. After the "STOP" card goes up, there shall be a 15-second grace period. Upon completion of the additional 15 seconds, the timekeeper shall stand and keep timing until the performer(s) is finished.

    c. Any performance in excess of the 15-second grace period shall not receive the First Division rating or the "I" ranking in the round.

3. If no official timekeeper is present, no penalty shall be enforced. **THE JUDGE SHALL NOT SERVE AS OFFICIAL TIMEKEEPER.**

JUDGE'S COMMENTS

Contestant:_____School Code:_____

Round: I   II   III   Finals

Impromptu Speaking

Rules: An impromptu speech is serious in nature with topics varying from round to round. Speakers will have a maximum of five minutes preparation time and a maximum of five minutes to speak. It is at the judge's discretion to drop rankings for going overtime. Limited notes are permitted. Students are to choose one from three topics offered.

Standard Evalutation:
1. Impromptu should identify a thesis and develop it using a variety of examples to support the thesis. (ie Personal, Political, Social, Historical, etc.)
2. Impromptu should be organized in a coherent manner.
3. Impromptu should be delivered using appropriate language and vocal/physical presentation skills.

_____

Please provide comments to help students:
1. Improve future performance in impromptu rounds.
2. Understand his/her ranking.

Feel free to use back of page if needed.

RANKING: Please rank the speakers from best to worst. Circle the appropriate number. No ties allowed.

(First)   1   2   3   4   5   6   7   8   9   (Last)

RATING: Please circle the appropriate number.

Superior   Excellent   Good   Fair   Poor

25 24 23 22 21 20 19 18 17 16 15 14 13 12 11 10 9 8 7 6 5 4 3 2 1

Please Sign:_____
        Judge name   code

Glossary of Terms

ABSTRACT RANDOM — A judge who is a people person, responding emotionally to a speech.

ABSTRACT SEQUENTIAL — A judge who prefers a rational, intellectual speech.

ACTING CHAIN — Talk, listen, react.

ANALYSIS — Results of a study of the elements of a character.

ATTENTION GETTERS — Openings for speeches that may include analogies, political cartoons, a shocking statement, a famous quotation, real or hypothetical stories, or humorous anecdotes.

BLOCKING — Movement that is theatrically correct and develops the scene and characters rather than distracts from them.

BRAINSTORMING — Creating speech topics in a spontaneous manner.

BROWSING — A method of searching for speech topics, especially useful for expository.

CHARACTER BLENDING — When a performer plays more than one character and the individual characteristics of a character mix with another.

CHRONOLOGICAL PATTERN — Answering an extemp question by looking at the past, present, and future aspects of an issue.

CLIMAX — Decisive turning point in the story.

CLINCHER — A pertinent ending to a speech, usually unifying the speech by referring to the opening.

CONCRETE RANDOM — A judge who makes intuitive leaps and likes open possibilities.

CONCRETE SEQUENTIAL —A judge who prefers a practical, real world speech.

CONFLICT — Struggle or disagreement.

CUT FILE — A box or crate containing file folders of information on extemporaneous topics.

CUTTING — A selected section of a larger work.

DELIVERY — The manner in which one communicates to an audience. Elements of delivery include the use of voice and body in the communication process.

DISQUALIFIED — To take away the right of further participation.

DRAMATIC INTERPRETATION — A memorized presentation of a serious or contemplating subject that is presented within a limited time and with limited movement.

DRAMATIC TIMING — Use of a variety of delivery rates for emphasis.

DUET ACTING — Two performers select a scene from a published work, develop characters, block the scene and memorize it for competitive presentation.

DUO INTERPRETATION — A memorized acting exercise performed by two students from a work of literature.

EMPATHIC RESPONSE — Pulling the audience emotionally into your scene.

ENTHUSIASM — Showing a strong desire to communicate to the audience.

ETHOS — Aristotle's term for the audience's perception of the speaker's character.

EXPOSITORY — An original speech which provides instruction or new information to the audience.

EXTEMP PREP ROOM — Where extempers gather to draw and prepare speeches.

EXTEMPORANEOUS QUESTION — A question of fact, value, or policy that one answers in an extemporaneous speech.

EXTEMPORANEOUS SPEAKING — A spontaneous speech presented on a randomly drawn current event which the student has previously studied.

EYE CONTACT — Looking directly at one's audience.

FLUENCY — Speaking without hesitation.

FOCAL POINT — Specific areas of visual direction.

FREE VERSE — Rhythmic variety with no rhyme or a loose rhyme pattern.

GESTURES — A speaker's use of hand movements emphasizing important points.

HUMOROUS INTERPRETATION — A memorized presentation with a comic or entertaining subject that is presented within a limited time and with limited movement.

IMPROMPTU — A speech presented on a randomly drawn word or quotation with limited preparation.

IMPROVISED DUET ACTING — Two performers draw a limited number of topics, choose one and prepare a complete scene with a limited amount of preparation time (usually thirty minutes).

INCONGRUITY — Inappropriate or not in agreement — an element of comedy.

INFLECTION — The rise or fall of the pitch of the voice.

KERNEL — The central meaning or heart of an impromptu topic.

LIMITED PREPARATION — An impromptu speaking situation involving little time to prepare for one's remarks.

LOGOS — Aristotle's term for a speaker's attempt to appeal to the logical side of the listeners.

MONOLOGUE — A part of a play in which only one character speaks.

MONOTONE — Everything said at one pitch — no variety in pitch.

MOTIVATED SEQUENCE — A method of organization that combines problem-solution with steps to heighten motivation.

MOTIVATION — A reason that makes a person do something or act in a certain way.

MOVEMENT — A speaker's use of body movement to support transitions or develop characters.

NARRATIVE PROSE — No dialogue in the selection.

OBSERVATION — Noticing and mentally recording facts and events.

ORGANIZATION — The structure of a speech consisting of an introduction, a body, and a conclusion.

ORIGINAL ORATORY — An original persuasive speech on a universal problem.

PACE — The rate of delivery.

PATHOS — Aristotle's term for speaker consideration of the needs, wants, and desires of the listeners.

PERSONAL BUSINESS — Gestures or other movements that define the character i.e., wiggling a leg, picking at your nails, playing with your hair.

PHYSICAL EXPRESSION — The use of gesture, pantomime, and movement in events such as duo interpretation.

PITCH — The highness or lowness of the voice on a musical scale.

POETRY — Words in verse usually with a rhythmical composition. Sometimes the poetry is rhymed. Poetry usually expresses emotions or stories in a concentrated manner.

POETRY INTERPRETATION — An interpretative reading of a poem or a collection of poems unified by theme.

PREVIEW OF MAIN POINTS — A preview of main ideas presented in the introduction of a speech.

PROBLEM-SOLUTION — A speech structure used in oratory identifying a problem and offering solutions.

PRO-CON — Answering an extemp question by examining the advantages and disadvantages of a proposal.

PROSE — A published work without rhyme or meter — ordinary speech.

PROSE INTERPRETATION — An interpretative reading of either fiction (short stories or novels) or nonfiction (essays, journals, or biographies).

STAGE PICTURES — Positions of actors on stage.

STANCE — The way a person stands (posture).

SUBJECT — A broad area of possible speech topics.

SUBTEXT — Meaning that is not directly stated but is inferred by other statements.

TAG LINE — The final line of a scene.

TEXT ANALYSIS — Interpreting the character and mood of the selection through the lines of the character, of other characters and through the author's advice.

THESIS STATEMENT — An exact statement of the speech purpose or topic.

TOPIC — A specific aspect of a subject suitable to the time limits of a competitive speech.

TYPES OF EXTEMP INFORMATION — Magazines, newspapers, television news programs, and the Internet.

UNIFIED ANALYSIS — Answering an extemp question by providing a justification of one's answer.

VOICE DISTINCTION — Differences such as pitch, rate, inflection that distinguish characters.

Index

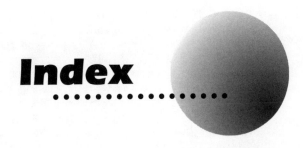

SPEECH CREDITS

ORATORY

Miriam Nalumansi-Lubwama
Original Oratory Speech (p. 162-165)
Reprinted by permission.

Natalie Foster
Original Oratory Speech (p. 165-168)
Reprinted by Permission.

EXTEMPORANEOUS

Doug Miller
Extemporaneous Speech (p. 169-171)
Reprinted by permission.

Ben Lerner
Extemporaneous Speech (p. 171-174)
Reprinted by Permission.

EXPOSITORY

Jennifer Liu
"What's In a Name?" (p. 175-178)
Reprinted by permission.   .

Sarah R. Bahr
"Just Left of Right" (p. 178-179)
Reprinted by permission.

All speech materials are copyrighted
by their respective authors.

TEXT CREDITS

Anthony Figliola
Excerpts from "Duo Techniques"
  originally published in **Rostrum**
  Magazine
Copyright 1996, Anthony Figliola
Reprinted by permission.

Robert Carroll
Excerpts from "An Introduction to
  Extemporaneous Speaking and
  Commentary" and "An Introduction
  to Impromptu Speaking" originally
  published in **Rostrum** Magazine
Copyright 1996, Robert Carroll
Reprinted by permission.

PHOTO CREDITS

Students of Wichita High School
  Southeast